MW00985664

Irish Paganism

Unlocking Pagan Practices and Druidry in Ireland along with Welsh Witchcraft and Celtic Spirituality

© Copyright 2022 - All rights reserved.

The content contained within this book may not be reproduced, duplicated, or transmitted without direct written permission from the author or the publisher.

Under no circumstances will any blame or legal responsibility be held against the publisher, or author, for any damages, reparation, or monetary loss due to the information contained within this book, either directly or indirectly.

Legal Notice:

This book is copyright protected. It is only for personal use. You cannot amend, distribute, sell, use, quote, or paraphrase any part, or the content within this book, without the consent of the author or publisher.

Disclaimer Notice:

Please note the information contained within this document is for educational and entertainment purposes only. All effort has been executed to present accurate, up-to-date, reliable, and complete information. No warranties of any kind are declared or implied. Readers acknowledge that the author is not engaging in the rendering of legal, financial, medical, or professional advice. The content within this book has been derived from various sources. Please consult a licensed professional before attempting any techniques outlined in this book.

By reading this document, the reader agrees that under no circumstances is the author responsible for any losses, direct or indirect, that are incurred as a result of the use of the information contained within this document, including, but not limited to, errors, omissions, or inaccuracies.

Your Free Gift (only available for a limited time)

Thanks for getting this book! If you want to learn more about various spirituality topics, then join Mari Silva's community and get a free guided meditation MP3 for awakening your third eye. This guided meditation mp3 is designed to open and strengthen ones third eye so you can experience a higher state of consciousness. Simply visit the link below the image to get started.

https://spiritualityspot.com/meditation

Contents

INTRODUCTION 1

CHAPTER 1: WHAT IS IRISH PAGANISM? 3

    A PEEK INTO HISTORY 4

    THE PAGAN LIFE OF ANCIENT IRISH PEOPLE...5

    THE DOMINANT PAGAN GODS 5

    PRIMARY BELIEFS OF IRISH PAGANISM 9

    ANCIENT ERA IRISH PAGAN BELIEFS 9

    MODERN-DAY IRISH PAGAN BELIEFS AND PRACTICES 11

CHAPTER 2: WHO WERE THE DRUIDS? 13

    THE ORIGINS OF DRUIDRY... 14

    DRUID HIERARCHY 15

    THE ROLES OF A DRUID 16

    COMMON DRUID RITUALS 18

    LINK TO HUMAN SACRIFICE 20

    HOW CELTIC DRUIDS SPENT THEIR DAYS... 21

    DECLINE AND REBIRTH OF DRUIDRY... 22

CHAPTER 3: PAGAN FEASTS AND FESTIVALS 23

    WHEEL OF THE YEAR 23

CHAPTER 4: CELTIC WITCHCRAFT AND BRANCHES OF BELIEF........32

    THE FOUR MAIN BRANCHES OF WELSH PAGAN BELIEF 34

THE FOUR BRANCHES OF MABINOGI 34

WAS WITCHCRAFT ACCEPTED? 36

THE HISTORY OF WITCH HUNTS 37

WHAT WITCHES LOOKED LIKE 40

PAGANISM VS. WITCHCRAFT 41

CHAPTER 5: IRISH SPIRITS AND DEITIES 43

DAGDA 45

MORRIGAN 46

BADB, THE CROW GODDESS 46

SUN GODDESS, MACHA 46

NEMAIN 47

BRIGID 47

LUGH 48

AENGUS 48

AINE 49

NUADA 49

GOIBNIU 50

DANU 50

MANNAN MAC LIR 50

BALOR 51

EITHNIU 51

CÚ CHULAINN 52

OGMA 52

CLIODHNA 52

CHAPTER 6: WELSH SPIRITS AND DEITIES 54

WELSH DEITIES 56

THE GODDESSES 56

THE GODS 59

WORKING WITH THE DEITIES AND ATTRACTING THEM INTO YOUR
LIFE 61

THE IMPACT OF THE MABINOGI AND WELSH MYTHOLOGY 63

CHAPTER 7: PAGANISM AND DRUIDRY TODAY 66

MORE THAN JUST A HOLIDAY 67

NEOPAGANISM 69

WICCA AND THE RULE OF THREE...70

CELTIC PAGANISM 73

CHAPTER 8: MAGICKAL TOOLS AND HOW TO USE THEM.................76

MAGICAL TOOLS..77

PAGANISM AND MAGICK...84

ANIMALS AND MAGIC 87

CRYSTALS AND MAGIC 88

PRACTICING MAGICK..91

HOW YOU CAN GET STARTED 92

CHAPTER 9: SETTING UP A PAGAN ALTAR 94

SIGNIFICANCE OF A PAGAN ALTAR...95

HOW TO MAKE YOUR PAGAN ALTAR 96

WHAT DIRECTION SHOULD A PAGAN ALTAR FACE? 97

CHOOSE THE STYLE OF YOUR ALTAR...98

ITEMS TO USE FOR THE GODDESS 98

ITEMS TO USE ON THE GOD SIDE 99

ITEMS TO PUT IN THE CENTER OF THE ALTAR 99

ADDITIONAL ITEMS TO PUT ON YOUR ALTAR...100

CHAPTER 10: SIMPLE PAGAN SPELLS AND RITUALS 102

BEALTAINE RITUALS..103

LOVE SPELLS 105

MAGIC 107

SPELLS FOR PROTECTION 108

HEALING RITES...109

CONCLUSION...110

HERE'S ANOTHER BOOK BY MARI SILVA THAT YOU MIGHT
LIKE 112

YOUR FREE GIFT (ONLY AVAILABLE FOR A LIMITED TIME) 113

REFERENCES 114

Introduction

Irish Paganism enjoys a long and rich history, originating from ancient Celtic religions and through numerous changes over centuries. In the modern era, more and more people with Irish Pagan roots have decided to explore their legacy, and with good reason. The spirituality-based Pagan Practices come in handy in times of need - whatever this may entail. Learning about the universal cycle of birth, death, and rebirth and venturing into different nature realms will guide you in all aspects of life.

Amid all the technological advancements and uncertain expectations of modern society, losing yourself is not unusual. The boundaries change all the time, and you have no control over them. The answer to all these problems lies in discovering your spiritual self. Modern Irish Pagan magick incorporates elements from various belief systems, so tapping into its wisdom allows you to find parts of yourself.

Apart from the historical aspects, this book explores the differences between the Irish and Welsh spiritual beliefs and magickal practices. Despite having the same roots, these two paths of Paganism have very notable differences. Many secrets will be unveiled, from how witchcraft was viewed in the two regions to the different branches both cultures have developed.

According to the Irish Pagan lore, we carry our ancestors in our blood, enabling us to communicate with them whenever we need their guidance. The innate appeal of this culture brings entire communities together during holidays on the Witches Wheel of the Year. The choice of becoming a solitary practitioner or performing spells and rituals with like-minded people should always be personal. However, many benefits are gained from belonging to an Irish Pagan community.

In Irish Paganism, the journey between worlds is also possible. However, acquiring this skill takes much time and effort. This fundamental knowledge will teach you many things about yourself and your magick. The Druids, Pagans, and even the Wiccans have done so for too many years to count. Now, you can do it too. All it takes is to unlock the secrets of their practices, and you can start your magical Pagan journey. You are provided with a practical guide of simple magickal tools and spells to take advantage of. Even people without much practice exploring their spirituality can take advantage of these tools.

This practice allows you to choose your spiritual guides, tells you how to approach them, and even the method to receive their messages. It all comes down to your tools and how you employ them during your spells and rituals. When you are versed in the fundamental parts of your craft, you are ready to grow your power even further, incorporating more and more of your background and beliefs and developing your unique magic practice.

Chapter 1: What Is Irish Paganism?

Celtic Paganism is typically an ancient religion with diversified practices and belief sets. The people who adhered to Paganism are widely known as Celts stemming from the Roman and La Tene periods. The British and Irish Iron Age carried much significance for Insular Celts. The oldest Celtic paganism records were written by Roman writers, whose personal hostile tendencies laid a particular biased hue on the historical records. Irish Paganism belongs to a larger category of polytheistic religions, and although there were many chronological and geographical variations between the finer details, there were also many structural similarities.

A Peek into History

Perusing historical manuscripts, you'll find that around 500 BCE, the Celts invaded Ireland. In essence, the Celts were practicing pagans and brought paganistic beliefs and rituals to Ireland.

Christian and other Abrahamic religious practices were at their peak during the Middle Ages, and ancient Celtic religious pagan practices were nearly extinct. However, Celtic religion was still alive in the Irish haven during this era, but the sources and written records existed in poems, usually written by Christian monasteries.

These historians were mainly ignorant of the gist of Paganism. Therefore, divine beings appeared as characters and heroes in the records instead of the pagan deities. One of the most significant examples of Irish records is Tuatha De Danann, depicted as merely an ancient human tribe. The Celtic belief was that Gods rest in the stars and worship the seasonal variations. However, as the core of the

Pagan religion, they were free to choose a god and feel united with the universe and nature.

The Pagan Life of Ancient Irish People

During the Paganism era in Ireland, the Irish were predominantly taught Druidic religion. The Druids were the most powerful and highly educated members of ancient society, with immense power over others. They were the only available preachers and teachers and were tasked with imparting knowledge to the children of kings or chiefs.

The Druids were royal court advisors, and people would turn to them seeking advice on important matters. According to historical records and reports, they had immense magical powers, able to raise a magic fog with the ability to hide specific things.

They were also believed to possess other magical properties, like manipulating the seasonal and natural world attributes. Several Irish folklore tales talk about similar exemplary powers exhibited by these Irish pagans. Although pagans were widespread across Ireland, the city of Tara was an exception. The vast majority of Irish pagans inhabited Tara because it was the dwelling of over-kings, and evidence that pagan roots ran deep in the heart of Ireland during ancient times.

The Dominant Pagan Gods

Although, the information about Pagan Gods is minimal since the tales about those Gods were never documented by the ancient Celts. However, the paganism spirit and their rituals or beliefs survived through folklores and some historical records. To better understand Celtic mythology, it is essential to learn about the intriguing details and great connections with their gods and goddesses. Discussed below are a few of the dominant pagan divinities honored by the people of Ireland.

- **Morrigan, The Goddess of War**

Morrigan is believed to be the phantom queen, translated to the queen of the demons. Merely thinking about Morrigan fills one with awe and curiosity. The ancient Celts thought she flew over battlefields in the shape of a crow and possessed the ability to foretell the battle's outcome. According to folklore, the deity Dagda was victorious in one of his most important battles because of her.

- **Aonghus, The God of Youth and Love**

The god associated with the valley near the river Boyne is Aonghus. He was the son of god Dagda and goddess Boann. Boann was the goddess of the River Boyne, and why Aonghus, also known as Angus, is connected to this river and valley. He was exceptionally handsome and believed to be the god of love and youth, able to evoke love in others, and had four birds circling him at all times. His life revolved around seeking a beautiful maiden.

- **The Pagan God Danu**

Danu had several names from Eastern Europe to Ireland, considered the earth mother goddess, and known as Dana and Anu. According to popular pagan belief, Danu is the one who nursed the gods. Perhaps because of these attributes, she was also known as the goddess of fertility and wisdom. In Irish lore, she is considered a highly skillful deity in magic. The Irish pagan lore also assumed that Dagda was her father; however, this story has various versions.

- **The Good Pagan God Dagda**

Dagda was a giant in stature and with a long and unruly beard. Popularly known as the good god, Dagda was a Celtic deity and considered the chief of Irish Tuatha de Danann. He always appeared as a fatherly figure, seemingly joyous and content. His superpowers were unique and not possessed by other gods and goddesses since he could give life and death. He was also associated with providing endless food and is also known as the god of agriculture. His children were Aengus Mac and Brigit from Boann and Morrigan, respectively. Dagda possessed vast skills and knowledge and was considered dominant over other gods. He could control seasons and provided endless food with the help of his cauldron.

- **The Pagan God Cuchulainn**

Cuchulainn was originally named Setanta, also known as the Hound of Ulster. He killed the dog appointed to guard Cullen and, after this act, was renamed Cuchulainn. People believed he could defeat death, as he was courageous in many battles, and why he declined Morrigan's gift of immortality. He did not consider it a favor because he had already defeated death several times. Morrigan, who hovered over battles as a crow, visited Cuchulainn when he died on the battlefield.

- **Fearsome Pagan Goddess Brigit**

As mentioned earlier, Brigit was Dagda's daughter and one of the most famous gods of pre-Christian Ireland. She was considered equivalent to the Roman goddess Minerva. Brigit had three central powers and attributes: the fire of the forge, fire of the hearth, and fire of inspiration. She was rightly known as the triple goddess, possessing diverse abilities and attributes.

• The Horned One, Cernunnos

As the name suggests, he was considered one of the most Celtic honored gods with very few other associations of his kind and connected to wild animals. Apart from wild animals, he was also linked to wealth and fertility. Not all the gods in the Celtic family are immensely represented through art, but Cernunnos was an exception and the reason he was easily identifiable and a popular god in Celtic ancient art.

• Arawn, the God of Underworld

God of the underworld or the dead is famous for darkness, fear, and his cloak. He was also known as the guardian of lost souls and a virtuous god. He represented war, fear, and terror. His biggest rival was Hafgan, who desired the position of god of the underworld or otherworld. It is believed that Arawn switched his place with Pwyll and defeated Hagan. Arawn rewarded Pwyll for this act of bravery with pigs.

• Abandinus, The Defender of Water

Out of all the Celts' ancient gods, very little information is available about Abandinus. Abandinus was the defender of the waters or seas. Most people associate this god with the inscription in Cambridgeshire, England.

These prominent pagan deities were quite popular in Ireland, and the gods and goddesses were thought to belong to the sacred tribe of deities. This tribe of gods and goddesses, known as the Tuatha de Danann, was considered the main Irish goddesses and gods tribe. The literal translation means "children of Goddess Danu." This particular tribe originated in the western islands and had the most magical powers, and the reason they settled in Ireland for so long.

Primary Beliefs of Irish Paganism

The beliefs of Irish Paganism are very humane and accessible, filled with kindness and an abundance of mysterious warm energy leading to great comfort. Irish Paganism's core belief revolves around love for nature and earth, overall harmony, and unity of the human community. It also greatly stresses being united with the universe.

Unlike the prevalent Abrahamic religions, Irish Paganism was a free-spirited religion advocated by beliefs in various gods. The pagan believers were encouraged to associate their subjective interpretations with the deities. Paganism proudly endorses three core principles keeping believers united across a common thread.

> 1. The first principle is about kinship and love for nature and others.
>
> 2. The second principle is about positive morality and advocates living your life your way as long as no one is harmed.
>
> 3. The third principle acknowledges and recognizes the divine (the feminine and masculine).

To better understand the Irish belief, it is best to discuss it from ancient and historical records and the modern perspective (which is more about neopagan spirituality).

Ancient Era Irish Pagan Beliefs

One of the most prominent resources often referred to in literature is Caesar's writings and records about the Gallic Druidism to the rich culture of Ireland. However, it may not be the most accurate depiction of what happened during the Irish pagan realm.

Interestingly, Ireland always opened its arms to soak in the traditions and culture of invaders and combine them with the existing culture. The result is an interesting and beautiful blend of cultures that created a curious cultural symphony. Some of the fundamental Irish pagan beliefs included the concept of "rebirth," revolving around the idea of the continuation of life in different cycles of birth and death.

The belief system in Irish Paganism signifies the importance of responsibility, honesty, loyalty, and justice – because without these attributes, an individual cannot be a good human being. This concept is among the most vital elements of pagan religion. They also believe in a "parallel world," which is nothing like an underworld but instead an entirely different world existing alongside this world. The Irish pagan folklore talks at length about the relevance and reality of this otherworld. The population of the otherworld consists of all beings, including goddesses, gods, royal or noble fairies (Sidhe), and elemental beings.

In addition to the belief sets shared above, Irish Paganism emphasized meditation and traveling between worlds. They firmly believed in occult power or hidden knowledge, and only certain people could develop these skills and could share them with others. Their belief included understanding and knowledge of prophecy, magic, and divination.

Even with rich religious beliefs and a firmly embedded pagan culture, Paganism shifted dramatically as Christianity gradually took hold. Over time priests replaced the Druids, resulting in various pagan beliefs' assimilation into Celtic Christian beliefs. The Celtic Christian Church was quite different from the Roman Catholic Church and advocated practices and beliefs not welcomed by orthodox mainstream Christian scholars.

As time passed, the pagan beliefs diluted even further as Christianity's influence became dominant. However, even with Christian dominance, Irish pagan beliefs survived. You can find numerous references to holy good observances (related to the pagan ritual of sacred spring and magic), crowds from the otherworld, Fairies or the Sidhe, etc.

Various folk practices and stories frequently refer to Irish Paganism resulting in several pure pagan beliefs and rituals surviving the sands of time despite the harsh and unwelcoming change. It brings us to the most recent era of Irish pagans. It is no wonder the modern pagan beliefs are nothing like the ancient ones, except for the essence still homogenizing and binding the pagan philosophy together.

Modern-Day Irish Pagan Beliefs and Practices

In today's surreal and chaotic world, Paganism appears to have acquired a prominent corner of solace for the Irish people. There is an innate appeal for pagan beliefs in Ireland, where a rich history of pagan religion still survives. Since 1970, steady growth in Irish Paganism, and although a few things have evolved, the change is subtle, and the primary ritual spirit and belief set is still in the original form.

These days the pagans organize a national Pagan Festival, the Feile Draiochta, for pagans to come together and recognize each other. However, because of the independent and tribal nature of Irish pagans, it is challenging to bring the whole community together. Moreover, non-profit organizations in Ireland are working towards advocating and promoting Paganism. The primary purpose is to safeguard the rights of pagan followers and spread awareness about the religion. Several monthly moots are for pagans to network and meet periodically to establish lasting connections and experience a healthy exchange of knowledge and beliefs.

As far as the pagan festivals and rituals are concerned, several are still celebrated by modern pagans. However, some ritualistic practices have subtly changed to fit modern life. The most famous Irish pagan festival is Beltane (celebrated on May 1) and Samhain (celebrated on

November 1). Modern-day Paganism is viewed as a reconstructed Irish pagan philosophy. However, reconstruction is not distorting the core beliefs and practices.

Since Paganism allows for individuality and subjective interpretation and construction of belief, many pagans nowadays define their rituals and practices. Some pagans practice a "stalking awareness," alert to their emotional and psychological state and the external world around them. Others find meaning in visiting pagan and Celtic spiritual sites and sites significant to other religions. In other words, Paganism welcomes a non-dogmatic and fluid ideology in religion and spirituality.

The principle of "polytheism" is at the heart of modern-day Paganism, honoring multiple goddesses and gods. The same belief was popular in the ancient era about females and males who embodied and related to different cultural aspects and natural forces. Worshiping nature is still popular and obvious because honoring nature is one of the foundational beliefs in Paganism and cannot be ignored.

Another core belief in modern-day Paganism is pantheism and animism, an integral part of this belief system. It's about the concept of entertaining a holistic worldview and interconnectedness. According to this belief, the spiritual or material universe and divinity are linked. Pagans believe nature is inseparable from divinity, with divine attributes spread around in nature (according to pantheism).

One of the central components of goddess-centered pagan witchcraft was understanding that everything in this universe is linked, like an organism. According to this belief, anything affecting one part has a ripple effect on the other parts. The other popular belief of animism was everything has particular spiritual energy or life force, or specific spirits are in the natural world, and it is possible to communicate with them.

It is evident that Ireland has a beautiful and strong pagan past, and, nowadays, a new wave of Paganism is growing stronger in Ireland.

Chapter 2: Who Were the Druids?

While most members of ancient Celtic societies were known as fierce warriors with a duty to protect their land and people, others had quite different roles. These were the Druids - a highly educated class of Celts occupying various leading positions in their society. Their primary role was as the repositories of their ancestors' accumulated knowledge, accrued since childhood. It was necessary to keep their traditions alive since the Celts would only pass on their wisdom through oral sources. It also secured Druidry survival, which is still practiced today, albeit in a modernized form.

The Origins of Druidry

Due to the lack of written records, the exact origins of Druidry cannot be determined with certainty. The few records we have on this practice come from the Roman Empire scripts and archeological findings throughout Europe. Regarding the Roman Empire scripts, these depictions of Druidry may be tainted by the centuries-long competition between the Romans and the Celts over European territories. However, since some archeological findings can be tied to the oral sources passed on by the Celts, it's possible to piece together some parts of the Druids' history.

The term Druid comes from the Irish word "Doire," meaning oak tree - one of the most telling natural wisdom symbols in Celtic Paganism. Druidry considers oak trees and the entire natural world a source of an immense power ready to be harnessed. Followers use this organic approach in their healing practices, along with the guidance they receive from the spirits. Some sources say that the same way Druids could heal, they could also inflict damage. However, this goes against the dogma of Celtic Paganism- which means it is unlikely to be true. Their knowledge of the earth and journeying between the realms was considered mystical. At the same time, their word was sacred among their followers.

The first reference to Druids comes from the 2nd century B.C. These accounts describe this Celtic class as a well-organized society. Not only did they have a hierarchy among their classes, but their life patterns also followed a natural order. Their life revolved around seasons, lunar, and solar cycles, and honoring the eight events on the Celtic Pagan calendar that coincided with these. Also known as the Witches Wheel of the Year, this calendar marked the most important celebrations in the Pagans' lives in Ireland and Wales. The Druids officiated ceremonies at Samhain (harvest festival), Yule (winter solstice), Imbolc (spring awakening), Ostara (spring equinox), Beltane (summer solstice), Lughnasa (first harvest), and Mabon (autumnal equinox). These holy days are repeated each year - as, according to the Druids (and Pagans in general), does nature itself.

Druid Hierarchy

Druids started their education in their early childhood and slowly gathered enough wisdom to perform all the prominent roles with which they were entrusted. They were taught by other, more experienced Druids, who had already accumulated a substantial source of knowledge during their life. This level of experience often took up to 20-30 years to achieve, so not all Druids could fulfill all the positions. Archeological findings show that many would wear clothes and headgear to emphasize their highly elevated status in their societies. Unlike the Celtic warriors, the educated class wore long robes and headpieces without a protective function. Due to the slight variations in these articles, it's also clear there was a separation between the different Druid classes.

For example, those with the highest ranks wore yellowish (once golden) robes and headpieces adorned with elaborate bronze carvings. They were typically teachers and other Druid masters with prominent roles. The novice was often discovered in dark robes and simpler headgear. Druids who acted as priests, healers, and advisors wore white, while those determining matters during battle wore red. The artistically inclined practitioners wore blue clothing. In some depictions, more experienced male practitioners also had long hair and an abundance of facial hair - another feature that separated them from the rest of the community. While the Roman sources deny the existence of female Druids, Celtic tales describe these women dressed similarly to their male counterparts.

Another proof of the hierarchy among the Druids is the traditional election of a chief Druid. Typically, this person was the most experienced and trusted member of their community, who - once chosen - held the position until the end of their life. They had the honor of deciding the most pressing matters concerning their clan and officiating the rituals during the main solstices. These leaders would also initiate Druid Masters and Teachers, responsible for carrying on their tradition. In many other societies, this separation existed because of the illiteracy commoners were afflicted with. In Druidry, it was due to the magnitude of the commitment required to master this craft.

The Roles of a Druid

Archeological findings and oral depictions agree that the Druids had sacred places for performing the most important rituals. Here, they would officiate deity worship, rule on all religious questions, and prepare for the major sabbats. These were secluded areas, like natural forest clearings and manmade stone circles. Stonehenge is a famous Druidic place of worship, a megalithic monument built around 2400 B.C. While it's unclear whether the Druids erected the structure, Stonehenge was a popular congregation site for Pagans during the major Sabbats. Today, this site is visited by Modern Pagans, Druids, and followers of other Neo Paganistic religions.

The Druids were seen as intermediaries between humans, deities, and spirits, so their help was sought whenever someone needed answers, guidance, or protection from malevolent entities. Druids were polytheistic and worshiped both male and female gods, meaning their practices were a true representation of the ancient Celtic belief systems in Ireland and Wales. Their offering could even appease the neutral spirits, so they weren't tempted to turn against humans. Due to this, many equated Druidry with the priesthood, calling practitioners Pagan priests. This knowledge was often reinforced because Druids were the most educated class among the Celts, and their opinion was considered sacred.

However, in reality, the roles of a Druid were wide-ranging. They would act as teachers, judges, scientists, poets, healers, and philosophers. They were respected because of their power to communicate with deities and spirits from all realms. Their rulings were also revered because of the infinite wisdom behind their abilities.

Not only were they knowledgeable about natural phenomena, but they could also explain supernatural forces. They were often asked to distinguish between the two and take control of whichever they faced. While they could not always control these events, they provided insight on how to protect against them - often saving the lives of their clansmen, animals, or crops.

It is also believed that Druids could foresee the future to an extent. They did this by interpreting certain omens and pondering about upcoming events. Eventually, this leads to them predicting the consequences. The Druids' aptitude for divination granted them the astronomers' function. Using their keen sense of prediction, they could prepare for any event on the Paganic Calendar and signal the rest of the community when it was time for them to do the same.

Their role as famous poets is well documented by the Romans and is evidenced by how Druids carried on their traditions to our day. Poets were not merely busy crafting songs and mystical tales - they were historians retelling the lives of their ancestors. The stories they passed on to the next generations were part of their folklore and represented the meaning behind their laws. These were lessons learned from ancestral experience or prophecies left behind by an even older Druidic culture.

When they weren't busy performing spells, rituals, and divinations regarding important political matters or healing, Druids tended to more common affairs. When acting as a judge, their roles included dealing with minor crimes within their community and even resolving conflicts between family members. A person could have easily been banned from religious affairs and even banished from the entire clan if the Druids considered this a necessary punishment. What's even more interesting is that the Druids could grant divorces to men and women, something quite unusual for ancient societies. Yet, for this Celtic class, every human soul was considered equal and, therefore, deserved equal treatment.

The Druidic monopoly on religious events went far beyond the realm of merely officiating them. They had so much power in their communities that anyone who disregarded their ruling in any matters faced exclusion from sacred rituals and religious festivals. If anyone dared to disobey them, they would be considered unclean, and their energy threatened to taint the entire event. Therefore, they had to stay on the community's periphery and were prohibited from even glimpsing upon an upcoming ceremony. In Paganic Ireland, Druids imposed certain prohibitions known as geis. While much more mundane than a punishment for a crime, a geis was considered a sacred taboo. Those who disregarded this edict faced many misfortunes, including the death of close relatives. While this also sounds like an evil act, the application of geis probably served as protection against illnesses and other inflictions. For example, individuals could be forbidden to eat the meat of certain animals Druids believed to be tainted with a disease - hence the death warning.

Common Druid Rituals

Apart from their most sacred places, Druids often hosted rituals and other ceremonies at natural sites of importance. Spring, rivers, lakes, hilltops, bogs, and three groves could all serve as a place of congregation for Celtic Druids and their communities. Here, the line between our realm and the Otherworld becomes thinner, particularly around Samhain and Beltane. This allowed the Druids to offer sacrifices to the spirit inhabiting other realms in exchange for protection and guidance.

When their clans were at war, Druids often performed animal sacrifices. If they did this after a battle, it was to express gratitude to the deities for victory or the small number of losses. The offering made before a battle was typically for divination purposes. The sacrificed animal was watched very closely, as any part of their death (or dead body) could offer a clue about the future. If there was any message about the outcome of the upcoming battle, the Druids were able to interpret it. While benign in nature, the Druids showed no mercy for the captured enemy.

On the other hand, the fallen warriors from their clan were given peaceful funerals, representing the ancient Celtic culture in the Irish and Welsh Druids' practices. They believed that when a soul left a body after death, it simply moved on to inhabit another body. Therefore, courageous warriors and leaders needed to be buried with a lavish ceremony alongside their most cherished possessions, including weapons and jewelry. Besides the burial ceremonies, the Druids also officiated cremations and excarnations. This ritual involved exposing the body to the elements until only the bones were left. The practitioners buried or kept these bones for future divinations and other ceremonies.

Like in many other Celtic Paganic cultures, using objects to cast spells or perform ceremonies was common practice in Druidry. When performing a healing ritual, Druids often needed to prepare potions to enhance their spells and possibly cure the ailment they were asked to remedy. The Druids' mystical association with dark magic and the ability to cast curses is probably the result of other religions trying to suppress this practice. However, the Druids did use natural remedies with incredibly powerful effects. They would go on trips to sacred grows at night to harvest herbs; only they knew where to find and use them properly.

Mistletoe was particularly often used in Druidic rituals among the Celtic Pagans in Ireland and Wales. This perennial plant was a traditional symbol of eternal life and fertility because of its ability to keep its leaves, even in winter. Mistletoe often grows on oak trees - which made its importance in Druidry even more pronounced. Due to its wide availability, this plant was used to cure various common ailments. However, its dosage had to be carefully adjusted. If misused, the plant had a poisonous effect that could lead to dire consequences.

The practitioners gathered below the tree to prepare rituals, feasts, and animal sacrifices. They would climb the tree to cut the mistletoe and place it on a golden hook before preparing it for the actual ceremony. A prayer was said to express their gratitude to nature and ask for whatever service was needed. This mistletoe gathering was typically done before a specific day on the Witches Wheel of the Year - before a sabbat or the sixth day of the moon. At this time, the moon hasn't grown to half its size, but it already possesses enough influence to ensure a favorable outcome for the ceremony to be performed.

Link to Human Sacrifice

While animal sacrifices were common among the Druids, it's unclear whether they offered human sacrifices. There are some testimonies about the Druids performing rituals requiring a human sacrifice. Other sources say they only participated in offerings made by other Celtic classes. Again, most of these records come from the Romans, who may have used human sacrifice as an excuse to diminish the value of Druidry. There is no clear evidence about which Celtic cultures were doing these rituals. Much of their work was viewed as magic with a bad influence on those outside the Celtic Pagan culture. Witnessing Druids perform a powerful healing ritual on fallen warriors may have led to some common misconceptions about their practices. Druids who acted as intermediaries between the clans were always in favor of preserving the peace, but they sometimes used unconventional arguments to persuade the chieftains to maintain good relations. Some of their words were often viewed as threats, which, again, led to exaggerations about their practices.

How Celtic Druids Spent Their Days

On a typical day, a Druid would wake up before the sun was visible on the horizon. They considered the rising sun's energy the most potent source of natural energy, so they used this time for divinations and gaining answers to pressing matters. This was typically done through an offering accompanied by a prayer to the chosen spiritual leader. Most Druids had a preferred way to communicate with a deity's spirit of their choice, which was unique for every practitioner. Depending on the answer they were seeking, the offering could demand everything from a simple gift to an animal sacrifice.

If a Druid served as a teacher, they would continue throughout their day telling tales of Celtic ancestors to children and other would-be Druids. Large numbers of young people would gather in front of them, waiting to be empowered with new wisdom, which, upon receiving, they held in great honor. Afterward, a Druid would consult with their clan chief about what they learned during their morning ritual. If they uncovered something concerning the clan's safety, the chieftain would ask them for their advice on the matter. If not, they moved on to discuss other important affairs, such as upcoming solstices, warrior oaths, criminal cases, conflicts with other clans, etc. Due to their infinite wisdom, the Druids were trusted to rule fairly on all matters and keep the community balanced.

Once all these matters were resolved, a Druid would take medicine to those who needed healing. They would also learn if anyone else required their guidance by interacting with their community. Arriving home, a Druid would prepare healing concoctions they needed to administer the next day. Late at night, they would ponder the issues they learned from others or prepare for upcoming rituals.

Decline and Rebirth of Druidry

Druidry played a fundamental part in Celtic Paganism, particularly in Wales. However, as the Roman Empire grew in strength, it eventually pushed the Celtic beliefs into the background. The Romans considered Druids a powerful binding force for the societies they were trying to take over, so they took it upon themselves to force it out as much as possible. Since Paganism emphasized spiritual values rather than worldly ones, Roman's early attempts to eradicate this culture weren't too successful. Unfortunately, this wasn't the case with Christianity - which during the medieval period, managed to render all the functions of the ancient Druids invalid.

They still managed to carry on their traditions. Some were forced to pass down their knowledge in total secrecy, while many Druids found a way to reach their followers by assimilating their teachings into the Christian practices. Due to their ability to adapt to other cultures, after the 17th century, Druids successfully revived their traditions. In modern times, Druidry is practiced somewhat differently than the ancient Celts, but its essence still lives on.

Like other remnants of the Celtic culture, modern Druidry represents a blend of ancient Paganism, Christianity, and modern Neopaganism religions, such as Wicca. In turn, other belief systems have also been influenced by this practice. For example, the number three, which was present in many Pagan symbols, and often used by Druids, is found in Christianity and Neopaganism practices. The circle is another symbol with great importance for the Druid beliefs and Neopaganism, and it still represents the circle of life and the wheel of the year.

Chapter 3: Pagan Feasts and Festivals

'Pagan' is a broad term used for many different groups, including the Wiccans, Celtic neopagans, Heathens, and others. Each group has its own religious beliefs, customs, and even languages. However, all these groups come together during festivities and celebrations at specific times of the year. This chapter discusses what makes the occasions so important for the different pagans and how the festivals are celebrated in the pagan culture.

Wheel of the Year

The pagan seasonal cycle is split into clearly defined moments throughout the year identified by changes in the seasons and the position of the stars. These different times are graphically represented through what is known as the Wheel of the Year. This circular depiction of the year divides the various celebrations into eight portions. Collectively these festivals and celebrations are known as Sabbath days/holidays. Four of the eight celebrations are of Celtic origin and are known as the Greater Sabbaths or the Quarter Days. The Greater Sabbaths are based on astronomical events, and for this reason, they can vary by a few days every year. The Minor Sabbaths are known as the Cross-Quarter Days, and these holidays are based on the solstices and equinoxes.

The solstices and equinoxes are changes in the tilt of the Earth and relate to season changes, and are determined by the way the sun's light hits the equator. As the Earth rotates around the sun, it also shifts forwards and backward on its axis, causing the change in seasons. If you are in the northern hemisphere, when the Earth shifts forward, you experience summer. When the Earth stabilizes and stands straight on its axis, this is the onset of autumn. When the northern hemisphere tilts backward and the Antarctic Circle faces forward, ahead of the Arctic Circle, it is the onset of winter. Also, while the earth is tilting sideways on its axis to one direction, it is also rotating irregularly around the Sun. It is like an oval circle around the sun, so we are very close to the sun at one extreme, whereas on the other end of the circuit, we are much farther away. This also plays a significant role in how we experience seasons and the intensity with which we experience heat and cold on earth during the summer and winter months.

The Wheel of the Year was an essential part of the Celtic and Pagan cultures as it was used to make sense of time – before calendars and clocks. With the Wheel of the Year, the Pagans could understand time and influence many life activities, such as what they grew and harvested, how they traveled, where they lived, and even their lifestyle.

Yule (Winter Solstice)

The winter solace is between the 21st and 23rd of December in the northern hemisphere and between the 20th and 23rd of June in the southern hemisphere. The winter solace is the shortest day of the year, accompanied by the longest night. In pagan traditions, this is the phase where the Child of Promise is born, the god that will overcome the darkness of the winter and guide people to a brighter, warmer, and fruitful spring. The days start to get longer, and the winter gets milder from this point on.

Yule is also closely tied to Christmas that Christians celebrate. Even though the Yule celebration has been part of Northern European culture since before Christianity, the festivals have overlapped and shifted from one to the other over time. For instance, the concept of giving gifts is common in both cultures. It is also a time to celebrate with the family, usually around a big feast. In Sabbath traditions, it is part of the culture to light a fire to Yule logs, whereas in Christianity, the tradition is to decorate trees. Pagans will burn Yule logs in their homes indoors and outdoors to bring good luck for the spring season ahead. Even the primary colors used in the Sabbath celebrations of Yule are commonly used in Christmas celebrations, such as red and green.

Pagans celebrate this time with sweet ale, hot cider, soups, and plenty of nuts and meat.

Imbolc (Candlemas)

Imbolc is a festive occasion built on the celebrations of Yule. This is celebrated on the 1st of February in the northern hemisphere, while the southern hemisphere enjoys this on the 1st of August. It is a festival signifying that winter is nearly over and warmer, more fruitful days of spring are just around the corner. This is when the last traces of winter start to fade. There is a lot more rain, and the sun and the Earth provide all living things with what they need to get back into the growth process.

In Pagan traditions, this is also known as Brigid's day, respecting the goddess Brigid. It is believed that if you leave an offering for Brigid, she will bless the harvest that is to come and save farmers from bad harvests. Since she is a god associated with growth and fertility, this is the most important time of year for her.

At the same time, this is a time for people to cleanse, just like how the Earth is cleansing itself of winter and refreshing for the year ahead. It is a time to sow fresh seeds, let go of the past, and be hopeful for a brighter future. If you want to make significant changes to your life and start anew, this is the time to do so.

The festival is highlighted by spring cleaning and making handicrafts symbolic of Imbolc. Using fresh spring flowers and eating fresh fruit is the norm at this time of the year.

Ostara (Spring/Vernal Equinox)

This is a special time of the year as it is the first time in the New Year that the length of the days and night become equal. In the northern hemisphere, this is celebrated on the 21st of March and on the 21st of September in the southern hemisphere. It is the pivotal point where the daylight hours start to increase, and we get a more positive vibe from Earth. There is plenty of growth during and after this phase transitioning into summer. For the pagans, it is the season of fertility. There is new life in abundance, and it is a joyous time. Like Christmas, this celebration is also reflected in the Christian culture during the Easter festival. The idea of decorating eggs with the symbolism of chicks and baby rabbits (among other animals) is all meant to demonstrate the coming of new life and a new beginning. It is the opposite of the autumn equinox.

Some people like to act out the role of the god and goddess, depicting the romance they experience that leads them to conceive the Child of Promise. Also, the way the night and day become equal is reflected by the god of nature as his personality is split between his higher consciousness and primitive sexual desires.

Beltane (May Eve)

The famous fire festival, Beltane, takes place at the end of spring and the start of the summer season. The northern hemisphere celebrates this on the 1st of May, whereas it is the 1st of November in the southern hemisphere. Beltane is also known as May Day. It celebrates fertility as much growth and development in all life forms occur on Earth. This festival is highlighted by fire, so many events and celebrations have bonfires at the center of the party, or there is a dance or performance using fire. Another essential component of the Beltane celebration is the Maypole, used to depict the reproductive part of the celebration. A pole has ribbons or multi-colored threads attached to it at the top, and people hold onto the threads as they dance and run around the pole, braiding it into a beautiful pattern. Women make crowns from flowers decorated with ribbons and wear them as they dance around the Maypole.

Families celebrate this festival with their children by planting seeds of small plants in pots at home, making wishes, and sending them out into the universe by casting them into the fire. It is a time when people look forward to the harvest they will get after a nice and bright summer. In pagan tradition, this is the time of the year when the sun god visits earth to fertilize it and play his part in the growth process. It is also depicted through the goddess and the Green Man, who symbolizes growth and rebirth. It also illustrates how the god transitions from being driven by lust and the urge to reproduce to committing to a relationship and raising the next generation.

It is also believed that this is when the veil between the living and the dead is at its thinnest. Therefore, people think they can communicate with the dead. Also, farmers will seek protection for their animals by taking them to open pastures and walking them through two large fires. This is believed to rid the animals of impurities and protect them for the coming season.

Litha (Summer Solstice)

Litha is the peak of the Earth's growth season as summer gets into full swing. Even though it is one of the lesser Sabbaths, it is still a much-celebrated time of year. In the northern hemisphere, it is between the 20th and 24th of June and the 20th to 24th of December in the southern hemisphere. It is also the longest day of the year, after which the length of the day shortens once again. In religion, this is the day signifying that the Sun god has reached the peak of his strength and maturity. It is the end of his youthful era where he roamed free and carelessly. Now it is a transition into a more serious part of life where the Earth is growing from the seeds to plants, and some plants may even have started to flower and give fruit. The Sun god is moving to a more protective phase in his life.

The monument of Stonehenge is also an important part of this celebration. Two large stones are located outside the main circle of stones known as the Heel Stone and Slaughter Stone. These two stones channel the sun's rays directly to the center of the circle on this day. All the activities and festivities on this day represent the sun's power and that the Earth is also entering a more mature phase of its life cycle.

Lughnasadh (Lammas)

Lammas is one of the greater Sabbaths and the first of the three harvest festivals. The word *Lammas* means loaf-mass, whereas the other name, Lughnasadh, means the gathering of Lugh, representing that Lugh has transferred his power. In the northern hemisphere, it is on the 1st of August, and in the southern hemisphere, the 1ˢᵗ of February. It is the first stage of preparation for the winter months ahead. The sun starts losing its strength from this point onwards, and the days get considerably shorter.

Pagans believe that during Lammas, the god sacrifices himself to the goddess, and she slays him with a sickle. The god's blood spills onto the earth and gives the earth the energy to last till the next Wheel of the Year. In this way, the god also transitions from the god of light and life to the Dark Lord of death, which is his role in the latter part of the year.

It is celebrated by baking bread in the shape of the god and making other artifacts representing the god. Celtics believe that the Sun god Lugh transfers his strength to the grains they are harvesting, and when they bake this grain into bread, the transfer of power is complete, and his role comes to an end.

Mabon (Autumn Equinox)

Mabon is the second of the harvest seasons and is another signal that the summertime is fading away and that people need to prepare for the winter. The northern hemisphere celebrates this during the 21st and 24th of September, and in the southern hemisphere, it is celebrated between the 21st and 24th of March. Once again, the day and night come into balance and are nearly in equal proportion to one another. The concept behind this phase of the Wheel of the Year is similar to what Christians practice during Thanksgiving. It is a time to reflect on the journey of summertime, how the earth gave us what we needed to stay alive and has even given us the fuel we will use in the winter.

While the spring equinox represented sexual energy, the Mabon period is a mystical phase of the year. It is surrounded by reincarnation, the cycle of life, the wisdom of planning for the harsh winter months, and the journey from the womb to the tomb. The god also contemplates these different ideas and concepts and reaches a higher level of consciousness. At this point, the god reconnects with the goddess as his higher level of consciousness grants him access to the underworld. By now, the goddess is the queen of the underworld, and it is another stage in their union taking place in a very different setting.

Samhain (Halloween)

Samhain is a well-known festival in Pagan culture and the modern world. However, the rest of the world recognizes this as Halloween rather than Samhain. This usually occurs around the 31st of October to the 2nd of November in the northern hemisphere and around the 31st of April and the 2nd of May in the southern hemisphere. Again, this is when the veil between the living world and the spirit world is extremely thin, so it is usually associated with ghosts, spirits, and extraterrestrial activity. It is believed that the spirits from the other world roam the Earth freely on this night. Since the spirits are so close to us, many people believe it is the best time to practice magic.

Samhain is the last of the three harvest festivals. The word Samhain is believed to come from an Irish word that translates to "summer's end." This part of the Wheel of the Year is also the opposite of the Beltane festival. Where cattle were initially sent out to graze on pastures in Beltane, this is the time of the year when they return and are again received with great blazing flames.

Some pagans and Celtics also view this festival as the witches' New Year as it is the end of the cycle for that year. It is a time when people think about the year, reflect on everything that happened, and pay their respects to those who passed away. It is a time when people practice gratitude and look at life differently as they prepare for the hard winter climate. They thank the gods for how they helped the people to achieve the resources needed for the winter and focus on how they can get through the winter successfully. In the modern-day, this is not that difficult, but back then, it was an extremely challenging part of the year that required as much, if not more, preparation than what was needed to get the plants growing and the crops ready for the summer.

During the festivities for this occasion, people sacrificed animals to the gods to thank them. They dressed up in animal skins and wore various animals' heads.

The god united with the goddess in the underworld dies at this point. The Sun child that is yet to be born is becoming more mature. The Sun god will be born in Yule, the next festival, completing the Cycle of Life.

All the various festivals in the Wheel of the Year are roughly 6 to 8 weeks apart, so there is always something to expect. How these events are celebrated has also changed with time, and people in different parts of the world also celebrate them differently. Due to the differences in weather, availability of resources, and other restrictions, people have found new ways to celebrate these events. However, the spirit of the festivals still lives on. Moreover, different covens have their specific way of celebrating the same events, and people from different backgrounds within the Pagan umbrella also have their festivals. But the essence of these events remains the same.

Chapter 4: Celtic Witchcraft and Branches of Belief

Witchcraft was a popular practice among almost every culture in history. Traditionally, the practice could be defined as invoking special powers to take charge of individuals or events. Magic and sorcery are two elements typically involved in the process. While it is elucidated differently in cultural and historical texts, most people, especially in the west, have always held inaccurate stereotypes of witchcraft. It is often perceived as witches meeting at night to partake in rituals with the devil and conduct black magic. These beliefs were particularly reinforced during the 14th-18th century witch hunts. However, these false perceptions are not merely similar to reality.

There are three main implications of the word "witchcraft" in the modern English language. The first is the regular exercise of sorcery and magic worldwide. The second refers to witch hunts that took place in the West during the 14th and 18th centuries. The last connotation is the variations of the modern Wiccan movement.

The words witch and witchcraft come from the Old English term *wiccecraft*. *Wicce* referred to female witches, and Wicca was the masculine term. Although there are terms that mean the equivalent of witchcraft in other languages, such as *sorcellerie* in French, *brujería* in Spanish, and *Hexerei* in German, none has the same connotation. It means they can't be used to translate each other accurately. It becomes even harder as we move away from Europe and into Asian and African languages.

The main issue with attaching a definite meaning to the term witchcraft is challenging because various concepts and underlying themes come with the practice. These concepts and themes are not fixed, and they change according to the time and place in history. It is not easy to find cultures other than the Irish and Welsh, who share reasonable, and somewhat similar patterns of beliefs attached to witchcraft. Besides sorcery, diabolism, magic, religion, the advances of time, and folklore, always influence and merge with these beliefs. For instance, some regions strongly believe that a witch's superpowers are intrinsic, while others are convinced mystical practices are learned and developed by any individual.

This chapter paints a picture of Welsh witchcraft and Paganism. You'll learn all about what mystical beliefs and perceptions of witches were like in Welsh society. As mentioned above, there are numerous overlaps between Welsh and Irish witchcraft. Yet, there are still some prominent characteristics and beliefs linked to Welsh Paganism, which we will be discussing in more depth. In this chapter, you'll discover what a typical Celtic witch looked like, whether witchcraft was accepted and revered among community members, and if Paganism has always been associated with it.

The Four Main Branches of Welsh Pagan Belief

There are four main branches of Welsh pagan belief: The Gods of Annwn (the Welsh underworld), the Protectors, the Skilled ones, and the Skies and Seasons. These characteristics of Pagan beliefs were very prominent elements among their pantheon of deities. Although many peoples or tribes within the Celtic Empire worshiped their own deities, some of the gods and goddesses were common among many Celts because they brought with their beliefs as individuals moved and conquered other groups. For instance, the Irish, Scottish, and English versions of the Welsh deities we discuss in more depth in Chapter 6.

The Four Branches of Mabinogi

The Mabinogi, referenced on several occasions, includes four branches. In the 11th century, the Welsh mythology tales were combined after being passed on through oral tradition. The Mabinogi were kept in medieval manuscripts and stored in private family libraries. Early modern scholars made strong efforts to restore and salvage the Welsh mystical tales. However, we only have two main versions, along with a few scrapes of the rest to this day. In the 1970s, the works were finally recognized as secular literature, which is only fair considering they contained elaborate characters and touched upon a wide array of gender-related, moral, ethical, and political themes. The mythology, unsurprisingly, also contained incredible, fantastical imagery.

Each branch of the mythology encompasses numerous sequential episodes of a tale. Each branch is named after its deity protagonist, who we'll be covering in more depth throughout the following chapters. The names of the branches are Pwyll, Branwen, Manawydan, and Math. However, it's important to note that this is a relatively modern alteration, and the branches were not named in the original medieval manuscripts. Pryderi is the only common character in all four branches of the Mabingoni, even though he is neither a central nor leading character in any of the tales.

• The First Branch

Pwyll, the Prince of Dyfed, is the tale of Pwyll's mystical and heroic visit to the otherworld. It delves deep into his shapeshifting abilities. Duels, and virtue, are all elements that led him to the creation of a powerful alliance. Pwyll is courted by Rhiannon, the goddess he married to grant freedom in this mythology, followed by his newborn son, Pryderi, being kidnapped and rescued; Tyrenon, the lord of the Kingdom of Gwent, then fostered Pryderi.

• The Second Branch

The tale of Branwen, Daughter of Llŷr, follows the goddess Branwen's betrothment to Ireland's King. The king starts abusing her after he is insulted by Efnysien, Branwen's half-brother. A war instigated by the brother erupts and results in genocide. The dead bodies are resurrected, and the head of Bran, the giant King, somehow remains alive after his death.

Pryderi appears as a war survivor, and Branwen dies of guilt and heartbreak.

- **The Third Branch**

Manawydan, son of Llŷr, is the heir to the British throne and Branwen's brother. The war brings him and Pryderi closer, leading Pryderi to arrange Manawydan and Rhiannon's marriage. However, devastation looms in the land of Dyfed, and Rhiannon and Pryderi are suddenly removed from Manawydan's life due to a trap. Manawydan becomes a farmer and pleads for their release from the enchanted trap and the land of Dyfed's restoration.

- **The Fourth Branch**

Math, son of Mathonwy, the fourth branch of the Mabinogi, unfolds into a succession of treachery and deception. It revolves around the war with Dyfed and Pryderi's death, followed by a virgin girl's double rape and Arianrhod's rejection of an undesired son. Her magician brother, Gwydion, was the mastermind and creator of these happenings. He stirs in a synthetically incubated pregnancy with an artificial woman (Blodeuwedd). She gets involved in a deceitful love triangle that ends with a traitorous murder. Gwydion then embarks on a Shamanic journey for redemption.

Was Witchcraft Accepted?

We started the chapter by explaining how witchcraft is perceived as an activity involving magic and supernatural powers to harm others. While many people still carry these misconceptions about witches, this stereotype was more popular in history. In the modern-day world, many think witchcraft is a mystical healing art.

Despite the popularity of witchcraft at the time, many people went on witch hunts to catch the practitioners of "black magic." Witchcraft was highly associated with black magic in ancient times. However, this belief grew more and more prominent during the later Middle Ages, after Christianity became the primary religion and the Roman ideology more widespread. The church officially prohibited divination, and they declared ritualistic magic as heresy. This triggered the onset of witch hunts in Italy and Spain during the 1420s. The Friars instigated a state of panic by spiraling satanic conspiracies and blaming all misfortunes on witchcraft and its practitioners.

The growing power of the Catholic Church and Protestantism spiraled the second huge witch hunt in Europe. Protestants targeted all forms of witchcraft during the 16th century, suggesting that witches were misled by the devil, which automatically garnered the Catholic Church's response. The allegations heightened, leading to the most vicious witch hunts in recorded history.

The History of Witch Hunts

When we think of Europe's early modern period, we immediately think of the great scientific and cultural advancements made at the time. Despite the academic and technological strides, the people grew more and more religiously intolerant as mass hysteria had struck the continent. This all contributed to the tragic witch hunts that overtook Europe between 1550 and 1700. Individuals were not only accused of witchcraft but were also executed for it.

The history behind witch hunts, alternatively known as the "witch craze," is very profuse and intricate. However, it's suggested that social issues, religious conflicts, and matters of gender and class were perhaps the driving forces behind this horrid historical occurrence. It is believed that the execution and torment the alleged witches endured were closely tied to particular problems in society. They were mostly victims of political and religious schemes.

When the witch craze came about, Europe was heavily divided and undergoing a socio-economic crisis. At the time, the European population was growing exponentially, pressuring the little agricultural resources they had to survive. Religious groups had been at war from the mid-16th century, during a time when Europe was already ravaged after the Huguenot and the 30-year wars.

No one had taken up a real interest in witchcraft, or even cared about it (other than those who were practicing it, of course), before the late 15th century. This changed when Henricus Institoris published Malleus Malefic arum, which was a treatise on witchcraft, in 1485, garnering the people's attention. This book served as a comprehensive guide for hunting witches and persecuting them. It undoubtedly left a great impact on the following two centuries of the European witch craze. The book aimed to provide a deeper understanding and a solution to the issues surrounding witchcraft at the time. It investigates the nature of the accusations of witchcraft, the trials, and Society's attitude toward women. The book remains one of the most prominent hallmarks of the history of witchcraft.

The church's main aim was to replace public beliefs with Christian ones. However, when it failed to eradicate the folk beliefs of the people who typically remained half-pagan, horror stories about the alarming practice of witchcraft and the potency of black magic were spread all over the continent. At the time, many people were practicing alternative medicine, which encompassed using charms and cures. This is the "magic" the authorities, and the church considered "sage and un-alarming." However, non-medicinal magical practices were deemed sorcerous and, therefore, heretical in the 15th century.

Christians began to grasp a sense or idea of witchcraft as a concept at this point, encompassing demonic and satanic worships, curses, harmful black magic, and Black Sabbaths. It led everyone to believe that folk activities and religious practices, particularly widespread in European rural areas, were associated with sorcery and the Devil. Ultimately, practitioners of folk religion, regarded as a satanic practice, were punished and criminalized. What further fueled these beliefs is that there were some malicious and widespread magical practices in these areas. Many individuals cursed others, which was evident behavior that cruel witches existed.

The tolerant and accepting individuals of the 15th century decided to take action. Anyone who wouldn't comply with the standard beliefs, systems of faith, and religious practices was marginalized. They were also terrorized and punished by other (typically the elite) members of society. During the 1500s, there was a popular notion that witches were part of a conspiracy and aimed to hurt Christians. People believed that the sorcerers had allied with the devil to eliminate Christianity. Many of the greatest Renaissance philosophers were convinced of the powers of occultism and magic, urging the elite to take matters seriously.

The Hussites and Cathars, along with other heretical groups of the time, were also put to rest by the Church before shifting its attention to the witches. In the 16th century, panic regarding sorcery struck Europe. The church's actions were sequential - they always followed a clear-cut pattern of some sort. For instance, an incident that gave rise to (typically unfounded) suspicions surrounding a person or a group occurred. Lower-class individuals, already marginalized and shunned, were most vulnerable to the accusations, and were the target group of the allegations surrounding witchcraft. Unsurprisingly, these allegations were made on false pieces of evidence. The accused were tortured in the hopes of getting a confession out of them before they were even trialed.

The trials were seldom fair, anyway. Even if it were a false allegation, those who were accused of sorcery expected to receive a death sentence right away. We don't know precisely how many people died during the European witch hunt. However, it is suggested that at least 40000 individuals were executed due to the witch craze. Anyone deemed guilty would be burnt alive, drowned, or hanged. The authorities claimed that barbarically killing them was "a must" since it set an example for others who were inclined to follow in their heretic footsteps.

Researchers believe that the witch hunts came in two waves, as we mentioned above. The first was to suppress heresy and, eventually, turned into a way to shut down political rivals. By the 1650s, the aim was not as explicitly about sorcery and witchcraft as it was previously, leading to a decrease in the number of witch trials.

The second wave of the witch craze was perhaps triggered by the intense rivalry that existed between the Protestant and Catholic churches. There was a growing need from both sides to ensure people conformed to their religion. Social tensions resulting from economic and social changes, inflation, and warfare also played a role in fueling these hunts because the need to keep control over the people was stronger than ever before. The authority used the witch hunts to threaten the lower classes, warning them against rebellion. Women, unfortunately, were the main victims. While some men were accused of witchcraft, women accounted for the greater number of allegations and executions because more women were becoming single, increasing societal tensions.

What Witches Looked Like

We don't believe there is a solid description of Celtic witches because they tried their best to blend in, considering they were being hunted. However, it is said that worship practices of Dionysus included drinking, feasting, animal sacrifices, and underground meetings in the Greco-Roman civilization. Horace, Aeschylus, and Virgil, among the most popular classical authors, also depicted sorceresses and witches as they illustrated harpies, furies, and pale-faced ghosts, dressed in decaying clothing with crazy hair. They also suggested that witches gathered at night and conducted human and animal sacrifices. During the late 20th century, Christians also accused witches of sacrificing children.

During the witch hunts periods, brutal practices were conducted on alleged witches. They used to prick them to find out if the Devil had made them indifferent to pain. They also searched them for the "devil's mark," which was thought to be anything that resembled an odd-looking wart or mole. They also threw the alleged witch into the pond. If the body sank, it was considered innocent because the water accepted it.

Paganism vs. Witchcraft

Wiccan beliefs started regaining popularity during the 1950s. The newly perceived religion started gaining more traction. However, unable to grasp what the practice of Wicca involved, many people confused Paganism with the new movement.

Witchcraft is highly associated with Wicca, a nature-oriented belief system. It includes rituals eminent during pre-Christianity times. In contrast, pagans, according to definition, are members of spiritual, religious, or cultural communities. Their practice revolves around the worship of the earth or nature in general.

Wicca, as a religion, can be traced back to Gerald Brosseau Gardner and England in the 1950s. Gardner spent a few years working across Asia before releasing the book *Witchcraft Today* in 1954. He started a movement built on pre-Christian traditions. It was based on three main aspects: respecting nature, magic, and worshipping a goddess along with other deities.

Pre-Christian traditions and rituals shape today's neopagan movement. Having a deep respect for nature is also a significant element of Paganism. This movement goes as far back as the 1800s before it was reshaped in the 1960s. It became a revival of fertility worship and nature. Pagans come from various belief backgrounds that particularly focus on equality and nature. They typically worship numerous deities. However, it all comes down to the practitioner's preferences.

It means that Wicca is different from Paganism but a subtype. As you know, there are many misconceptions about what it means to be a pagan or a Wiccan, and people typically mix both with each other. While technically all Wiccans are pagans, not all pagans are Wiccans.

In short, modern-day Wiccans are regarded as present-day witches. The aspect of magic is what sets Paganism and Wicca apart. While Wicca is a subcategory of Paganism, they share the core elements of fertility, nature, and spirituality.

The answer to the age-old question, "Is witchcraft real?" depends on many factors, including personal beliefs and the connotations attached to their time and place. Even though there is no solid definition, one thing is for sure, the depiction of witchcraft in literature, movies, and art is not at all representative of reality.

Chapter 5: Irish Spirits and Deities

Irish mythology encompasses details of ancient Ireland and the origin stories of deities, heroes, and kings. Among all the branches of Celtic mythology, ancient Irish beliefs and mythology are the best preserved. These ancient beliefs were passed down from generation to generation until the Middle Ages when Christian monks started writing down the narrations and placing them into historical records. The tales of ancient Irish beliefs and traditions might have evolved, but the deities and characters remain the same. Most Irish folklore and tales are chronologically placed into four cycles: the Mythological Cycle, Ulster cycle, Fenian cycle, and the Historical Cycle.

The importance of deities, gods, and goddesses varies a lot. Dindshenchas is an early Irish literature class focused on the origins of Irish mythological characters, places, and related geographical events. In comparison, most historical records hold great regard for warriors, heroes, and revolutionary leaders. Early manuscripts and texts like Dindshenchas emphasize the divinity of ancestors and goddesses. These primal deities are regarded as the region's ancestors and are deeply rooted in the land's sovereignty. Similar in attributes to Greek and Roman gods, Ireland's primal deities are immortal beings fostering various attributes that define their character. Many Irish deities portray human-like qualities of greed, anger, weakness, jealousy, etc., whereas others are linked to natural phenomena on earth. There are even Irish deities possessing the ability to transform their physical appearance.

In this chapter, we explore the realm of Irish deities, read about their personalities, and understand how to work with these deities and honor them.

Almost all Irish gods and supernatural beings are related to the Fomorians, Tuatha Dé Danann, and the Fir Bolg. The Tuatha Dé Danann maintained a positive image among these early descendants, whereas the Fomorians exhibited mostly negative, revolting, and gruesome characteristics. The Fir Bolg was the third race to inhabit the region but were eventually overthrown by the Tuatha Dé Danann, accepted as divine beings or gods having powerful skills and supernatural abilities.

According to folklore, the Tuatha Dé Danann were perceived as supernatural beings proficient in practicing Druidism, history, prophecy, and magic. The <u>Book of Invasions</u>, written by 11th-century monks, explains Tuatha Dé Danann as godlike beings in the form of humans who disappeared after the Milesians arrived. Some accounts say the Tuatha Dé Danann chose the underworld after leaving Ireland, while others propose the Tuatha Dé Danann blended in with the early Irish ancestors.

Here are a few key deities, warriors, and spiritual beings from Irelands' mythological past without further ado.

Dagda

Dagda, or the good god, is a key deity in Celtic Mythology and is portrayed as a chief god of the Tuatha Dé Danann. He is considered a leading figure with influential Druidism, kingship, and super-human strength characteristics. Manliness, strength, wisdom, fertility, and magic are attributes associated with Dagda. He ruled as the king of Tuatha Dé Danann and controlled life and death, weather, and agriculture. Accounts of Dagda from Irish mythology describe him as a bearded giant carrying a long staff called long mór and the ability to restore life. He also carried a bottomless cauldron that never ran empty, and a harp called "Daur da Bláo," which gave him the power to influence emotions and the weather whenever he played it. Dagda is often associated with the famous Celtic Goddess Morrigan and is the father of Aengus, Bodb Derg, Midir, Brigit, and Ceramic. You can gather several things around your altar to honor Dagda, including offering butter, pig meat, and porridge ale. Resembling the cauldron of Dagda, place one cauldron at the altar and fill it with produce and related food items to express your gratitude. As Dagda showed compassion towards others, you can honor him by helping others or donating to demonstrate generosity.

Morrigan

The wife of Dagda, Morrigan, has many titles like the queen of demons, phantom queen, and the goddess of war. The queen possessed the ability to transform into a raven and hover over the battlefield – as well as the ability to predict the outcomes. Tales also tell of Morrigan having enough power to influence whether one would triumph or die during a battle. Despite being associated with war and battle, Morrigan is held in high regard as having the rightful kingship of the land. Her tales from the accounts during the Ulster cycle depict her shapeshifting into a cow or a wolf. Some neopagan traditions have painted a negative picture of Morrigan by associating her role as a destroyer. However, many scholars don't agree with the portrayal and connect her attributes to sovereignty and generosity.

The Morrigan is regarded as a triple goddess as different texts refer to her by different names. Some historians also suggest the three names of Morrigan could be three different personalities having similar attributes. Here are the three personalities associated with Morrigan.

Badb, the Crow Goddess

Badb is portrayed as a fierce goddess influencing the battlefield. She can shapeshift into a crow, appear as an old woman, influence destruction, and convey prophecies. Her presence is heard as the flapping of large wings over the head. Badb is linked to the Crone aspect of the triple goddess.

Sun Goddess, Macha

Macha is often associated with motherhood as she is associated with sovereignty, love, and prosperity. Legends say the union of Dagda with Morrigan helped the land as she granted prosperity to the area after the union.

Nemain

She is the sister of Badb and has somewhat similar attributes, which influence the battlefield. Nemain translates to a dose of poison as she can cause chaos, confusion, and frenzy on the battlefield.

Study the goddess of war's characteristics, the three personalities she is portrayed as, to honor her. The more you study, the easier it will be to work with the deity. When setting up the altar, focus on placing items linked deeply with the Celtic heritage. You can offer her red wine, crow feathers, mead, and red foods. Place her statue or a picture, including candles and decorative items representing animals like deer, crows, and cows, on your altar. People with a higher degree of knowledge and expertise also perform shapeshifting rituals, crow magic, and shadow work to build a better connection with the deity.

Brigid

She was the daughter of Dagda and revered in Christianity as St. Brigit. According to the written tales, she has two sisters called Brighid, and each is associated with a unique ability. The three sisters are seen as a single deity possessing aspects of healing, agriculture, fire, prophecy, and poetry. Folk stories tell of Brigid possessing a green mantle that carried the power to heal and comfort the sick or distressed. Imbolc is a festival celebrated to honor the goddess Brigid, and devotees honor her to get her blessings.

To work with Brigid, dedicate a space to the deity and honor her with simple items like her representation, water, and candles. When you burn the candle, dedicate the flame to her as she kept the fire burning in ancient times and use it to connect with her. When honoring the healing aspect of Brigid, find a natural water source and ask for her blessings.

Lugh

Lugh is one of the top three deities in Irish mythology and the son of Cian and Eithne. Later records perceived him as a warrior and historical figure. Lugh was the chief of the Tuatha Dé Danann and played a vital role in introducing the civil aspects of the mythological period. He carries the Sleá Luin Lugh, a sacred treasure, and has a hound that fights alongside him during battle. He is an all-seeing deity possessing several characteristics like a craftsman, warrior, seer, and poet.

By honoring gods and goddesses, we build a relationship to seek their blessings and guidance and connect with them. Read ancient texts to understand the personality of the deity Lugh, as it will help maintain ritual purity. Lugh possesses musical skills and is attracted to music and related expressions while praying. You can offer food items like bread, butter, milk, and fruits to the deity to seek blessings.

Aengus

The God of love and youth, Aengus or Aonghus, is the son of Dagda and the goddess Bion. Folk tales depict him in his search for a maiden. The story tells that he searched all over the region until he found the maiden accompanied by 150 other maidens who were to be turned into swans. The legend says that Aengus transformed himself into a swan to be with the maiden he adored. Aengus is compared to the Welsh god, Mabon ap Modron, who has a similar personality. The Celtic god had a horse with magical powers to carry an entire household on the back. He wore a multicolored cloak that reflected only one color to the person struggling between life and death.

Besides having attributes of love and youth, Aengus could resurrect the dead using his breath of life. His shapeshifting abilities allowed him to turn into a swan and be depicted as a youthful man. To honor Aengus traditionally, use dairy products as an offering. Baked food items, cheese, mead, cooked water bird, and honey are other food offerings you can choose.

Aine

Praised as the goddess of fertility, love, sovereignty, protection, and warm summer, Aine is a powerful deity with multiple roles as the Sun and Moon goddess. She is believed to teach her people the true meaning and expression of love. Besides the above-mentioned attributes, Aine is associated with fertility, livestock, prosperity, abundance, and wealth. Lady of the lake and the Feary queen are two popular names given to Aine over time. The hill of Knockainy in Limerick County is linked to the goddess. With her two sisters, Fenne and Grianne, she is categorized as a triple goddess and a complex entity with whom to work.

During the summer solstice, or *Litha,* the goddess is most present, and an opportunity to connect with her. Summertime is the most feasible as her presence is not felt much in winter because she is less active. As a goddess of love, and fertility, she has the power to attract or cause harm to an unwanted adorer.

Make a dedicated space for the deity on the altar and include decorative pieces representing a horse, swan, or rabbit. Placing horseshoes are also a good option to consider. Incorporating music into the rituals assists in better connecting with the deity since she played the harp. The food offerings include meadowsweet, grains, corn, lavender, honey, and, in some rituals, menstrual blood. Most deities, including Aine, are best invoked during the full moon because it is associated with the motherhood of the goddess.

Nuada

Nuada was the first king of the Tuatha people and one of the founding fathers of the Irish region. He was a skilled fighter, warrior, and hunter who arrived in Ireland and claimed the land from the Fir

Bolg. Nuada lost his arm during the battle and became ineligible to be on a throne. He possessed a sword called the sword of light with a blade sharp enough to leave his enemies in half.

Set up the altar and connect with him by offering basic elements of air, water, and fire. As the deity specializes in war and weaponry, you can seek blessings to improve courage, determination, and guidance to do justice.

Goibniu

Referred to as the smithing god of the Tuatha Dé Danann, Goibniu also possesses hospitality qualities. He was the first to work with metals and made weapons for his people. Most texts suggest that he worked alongside his two brothers. He made a silver arm for Nuada. Besides his smithing abilities, he possessed a cow who produced great quantities of milk. Goibniu is a deity who prepared feasts for the gods, and his prepared meals, when offered to warriors or the sick, protected and healed them from decay and illness.

Danu

Danu is a mother goddess of the Tuatha people and an ancestor of the Irish region. The goddess is linked to fertility, wisdom, regeneration, and strength but early mythological texts have limited literature available about Danu. She was perceived as an important character by modern scholars who wrote texts after the introduction of Christianity into Ireland. The Celtic goddess is described as a beautiful woman and was the divine mother of the people.

Mannan Mac Lir

Known as the god of the sea, Mannan Mac Lir is a popular Celtic god who ruled the seas and was revered as the master of illusions. Mannan Mac Lir fostered his blessings and belongings to Lugh. Here's a small list of his possessions:

- A steed named Finbar could travel over land and sea

- A boat called an *ocean sweeper* that traveled according to the thoughts of the one who sailed and did not require sails, an anchor, or the relevant equipment to navigate the boat

- The cloak of mists changed color depending on the mood of the wearer. Stories tell that the cloak made thunder-like sounds whenever Lir got angry.

Some other belongings included a sword sharp enough to cut through armor and a spear.

The Manx people regarded Mannanan with great honor and sought his blessings. They offer the god rushes as tributes during the summer solstice.

Balor

He is a member of the Fomorians and a striking figure. Most Fomorian gods portray a negative character and possess destructive powers. Balor is depicted as having a human body with the head of a goat. The forehead has a third eye that can wreak havoc on anything in the surroundings. A legend suggests that when Lugh killed him, Balor fell face down on the ground, and his evil eye was open, which created a deep hole in the earth. The lake of the eye in Co Sligo is referred to as the hole made by Balor's evil eye.

Eithniu

Eithniu was Lugh's mother and the daughter of Balor and was locked away as she foretold her son Lugh would kill Balor. The stories suggest she was rescued and gave birth to three children, one of which was Lugh. Balor tried to drown the three kids, but Lugh survived and was raised by the sea god Mannanan.

Cú Chulainn

Cú Chulainn is a powerful deity talked about in the Ulster cycle. He is a heroic fighter and recognized as the greatest warrior of the region during his era. Cú Chulainn is believed to be a demi-god with supernatural abilities. He had unparalleled athletic abilities and could even handle sedating potions that would take an average person a day to overcome. The rage he portrayed during the battle made him undefeatable. Cú Chulainn used a slingshot called Gae Bolga, similar to a spear covered with deadly thorns.

The strength Cú Chulainn possessed was bound by two rules he had to follow at all times. He was forbidden to eat dog meat and always had to accept food offered by a woman. Ancient texts depict him as a youthful and beardless man popular among the females for his beauty.

Ogma

Oghma is another member of the Tuatha Dé Danann associated with intelligence, learning, and expressiveness. Besides these amazing abilities, Ogma was a great warrior and fought side by side with Lugh. He is portrayed as having long chains of gold and amber attached to his tongue that pursue the followers. He invented and introduced writing into the Irish region. As a warrior, Ogma possessed a sword that kept an account of his heroic endeavors and could recall on command.

Cliodhna

She had many faces and was called the mermaid, fairy queen, and witch. Cliodhna was the queen of the banshees and linked to beauty and love. She possessed an enchanting power to heal the sick. Three birds traveled with the goddess and sang songs that could heal anyone. Written mythological accounts say that whoever listened to the songs would go into a deep sleep state and wake up fully recovered from the illness.

A famous myth regarding the goddess is that she fell in love with a mortal man named Siobhan and wanted to leave the underworld to be with her lover. However, the other gods lured her into sleep and sent her back to the otherworld. Being depicted as a queen of banshees, she lived in cork alongside other fairies and turned into a banshee when an Irish ancestor died. In some texts, it is believed that Cliodhna became a witch after the spread of the church.

Working and connecting with Cliodhna can be a magical and unique experience for people practicing Paganism. Start by reading and understanding the goddess's stories, legends, and folk tales. Her representation at the altar is necessary alongside items like seashells, driftwood, shark teeth, plants, stones, and related elements. You can offer her fruits, vegetables, cakes, mead, and water as an offering.

Chapter 6: Welsh Spirits and Deities

Mythology is an important aspect of life for several good reasons: it makes up a significant portion of our heritage. Mythology always reminds us of who we are, where we belong, and where we come from regardless of our geographical location or what we've achieved in life. Each culture and civilization has its unique set of mythology, legends, and folktales. It's incredibly amazing how these myths have a lot in common and act as a unifying force, even though they each tell different tales and comprise different deities and characters. Our ancestors all used folktales and mythology to make sense of the world around them, regenerate their sense of purpose, and establish a system.

What is mythology exactly, though? By definition, mythology is a half-truth or a complete fiction that makes up an aspect of an ideology. It is a historical story that explains traditions associated with a particular culture, civilization, or group. These myths are typically cosmological and cover events – and even battles – between the deities. Some cultures also have mundane mythology that revolves around normal people having a supernatural experience. Mythology has served as the stepping stone of storytelling for ages.

Mythology is a significant aspect of life for another very important reason, and it acts as a building block for many religions. They are also a foundation for many moral questions and issues. For instance, most myths and tales are about the struggle between good and evil. Every myth and ritual tells stories; the protagonist embarks on a journey that teaches him the necessary morals and personal values to overcome obstacles or defeat the antagonist. Like *The Odyssey*, some legends and tales are so great they have become literary classics for the entire world to enjoy and learn from.

If you think about it, mythology still plays a huge role in our lives. Besides the cultural norms and traditions we live by or sayings embedded in our culture, mythology is reshaped and takes on a new form every day. For instance, one of the most popular examples of modern mythology is comic books. Ever since the creation of *Spider-Man* in 1962, the tale surrounding Peter Parker's incident turning into the renowned Spider-Man has been passed down from one generation to the other. Some comic books and fantasy tales are even based on actual ancient mythology. For instance, Thor is inspired by Norse mythology, while *The Chronicles of Narnia* encompasses characters derived from Roman and Greek mythology. Other examples, like the *Harry Potter* series and *The Hobbit*, have become major examples of modern-day mythology.

This chapter covers many of the most prominent Welsh deities and spirits. You'll learn about them and their tales and discover the importance of Welsh mythology today and its influence in the modern-day world.

Welsh Deities

There are over 36 prominent deities in Welsh mythology, but we will cover the most significant ones. As you may recall from Chapter 4, many Welsh deities were widespread among all Celts. Also, there are equivalent gods and goddesses in Irish, Scottish, and English mythology. You may also remember Rhiannon, Pryderi, Branwen, Bran, Manawydan, and Gwydion from the tales of the four branches of the Mabinogi.

The Goddesses

- **Aeronwen**

    Many people believe that Aeronwen is the Welsh version of the Proto-Celtic goddess Agrona, and the Irish goddess Morrigan. Aeronwen is a Welsh goddess and deeply connected to fate. Agrona was the goddess of war, and the connection to Aeronwen is easy to see. They both determine how a battle would play out, each in their own way. As with most deities that determine how your life will play out, many sacrifices were made to Aeronwen. A battlefield, the number three, and the color black are commonly associated with Aeronern.

- **Blodeuwedd**

Blodeuwedd was Lleu Llaw Gyffes' (Arianrhod's son) wife. Most sets of deities have trickster gods, and that might have been Blodeuwedd. She liked to trick people, cheat them when she could, and go against her word – she even plotted to kill her husband. In modern times, she is seen as a beacon of female independence, the god who stood up against women being forced into a marriage that was loveless. Those who are single or in loving relationships will turn to Blodeuwedd for help.

- **Arianrhod**

Although we don't know much about Arianrhod, she is among the more popular Welsh deities. Her name translates to "Silver Wheel," a symbol of the moon and why she is the Welsh goddess of the moon. Don is Arianrhod's mother, and Lleu Llaw Gyffes and Dylan ail Don (the twins) are Arianrhod's brothers.

- **Branwen**

The deity Branwen is renowned for her beauty. She is the daughter of Llyr and Bran and the sister of Manawydan. She found herself in a loveless marriage to a partner who was abusive. Through the help and strength of her family, she was able to free herself from her matrimonial bond. In order to save her, sacrifices had to be made, and legend tells that a great war ensued, killing almost everyone. It was only the pregnant women who survived. Feeling guilty and heartbroken, Branwen also dies. The deity is regarded as a "protector of abused women." She is also the goddess of healthy, nourishing marriages and true love.

The Bedd Branwen Period was a period of time spanning 1650 BC to 1400 BC – part of the Bronze Age. When the riverbanks of Alaw were searched, a ruined grave was found, and it was believed that this grave belonged to Branwen. This gives more credibility to Branwen being a real person

- **Rhiannon**

Rhiannon is the Welsh Goddess of horses and strength. She is a topic of great interest in the Mabinogi and other Welsh mythology. The fae is a spiritual place where deities, spirits, and other beings are said to dwell. Before she came to our land, Rhiannon was a dweller of the fae – some suggesting that she was a princess of the fantastical world. There are many stories told about Rhiannon. She left the far to marry Pwyll, a great hero of the human world. She had her baby stolen and was blamed for many years until she returned to the fae later in life to prove her innocence.

Rhiannon did not shy away from her destiny or from facing her problems, and this gives inspiration to women (and everyone else) around the world. She would often ride a horse, and the horse has become a symbol that is closely associated with the deity. Because of the tragic story of her son, she has become a symbol of motherhood, strength, and love. She is often prayed to when people are entering marriages, seeking more in life, or wanting to know what is to come.

- **Cerridwen**

The Welsh goddess Cerridwen is popular among many modern-day witches and neopagans. She is an herbalist, witch, and the guardian of the cauldron of knowledge. Cerridwen is also a shapeshifting moon goddess. Afagddu and Crearwy were the son and daughter of Cerridwen, and her husband was a giant. Cerridwen brewed a potion for Afagddu, granting him knowledge far beyond anyone else. The magic did not only come from the potion – Cerridwen was extremely knowledgeable, and she passed that on to her son. She is prayed to for knowledge and wisdom or when performing magic.

- **Modron**

In the Celtic Wheel of the Year, Modron is associated with the Autumnal Equinox, known as Mabon (the Divine Child). She is the Great Mother of the Divine Child. Many claim that Modron and Rhiannon are the same deities, considering their stories' similarities. For instance, Mabon's child was kidnapped in the middle of the night, only to be returned after they endured so much punishment and suffering.

The Gods

Arawn

Annwn is the underworld or otherworld, and Arawn is the king of this world, protecting it and shepherding the souls that cross over. There is a story of Arawn paying for a misdeed by swapping bodies with the mortal Pwyll, a great human hero. While it must have been degrading for a deity to switch forms with a mortal human, they ended up becoming close friends. As Christianity swept into the land of Wales, getting rid of the "old ways," the title "god" was revoked from Arawn. The hunt has always been important in Celtic mythology, and many gods took part in the great hunt. Arawn took to the skies with the others when the hunt commenced, and he has become closely associated with not only hunting but the feast that comes after the hunt.

Bran

Bran is popularly known as the blessed Welsh god. He was a Celtic god whose name is translated into "raven." Many people claimed him to be a kind hero and a giant. It is also said that he was deified after his passing. Many legends illustrate him as Llyr's (the mighty god of the sea) son. The god Manawydan and the goddess Branwen were his siblings. Bran was killed following a brutal battle; he asked his brothers to behead him so they could carry his head back to the kingdom. The head communicated with his brothers until they put it on a hill where the current London Tower is located. The head was meant to face France to take care of any potential dangers. If ever the ravens leave, the head will no longer be protected, and the country might fall into peril.

Mabon

Mabon is the Celtic holiday that celebrates the arrival of autumn, the autumnal equinox. Mabon is also a god and is named after this holiday around this time of the year. Not only is Mabon known in other mythologies and religions by different names, but he is known in Celtic mythology by many different names. He is the Son of Modron and is considered the god of youth and rebirth. As we mentioned above, Mabon was kidnapped from his mother when he was only three days old. King Arthur plays a large role in the mythology and history of Britain. When Mabon became a man, Arthur's knights saved him. He is a man who is old but young at the same time, toeing the line between both, and he is most present on the equinox when night and day are equal in length. Mabon rides his horse with his hound by his side, protecting the beats of nature.

Hafgan

What would a set of deities be without a plot to kill another? Do you remember when we explained that Arawn switched bodies with Pwyll? Hafgan was always a rival of Arawn, and Arawn took his chance to remove Hafgan when the switch happened – Arawn asked Pwyll to murder Hafgan. After Pwyll's success, Arawn seized the throne and united the kingdoms into a sole otherworld.

Manawydan

Son of Llyr, husband of Rhiannon, and brother to Branwen and Bran. Manawaydan is often conflated with the god Manannan Mac Lyr, the god of the sea of the Isle of Man – they share some distinct similarities. Manawaydan helped secure Bran's head at the London Tower. This Welsh Celtic god is expanded upon into two of the Mabingoni branches. The third branch tells that he saved Rhiannon from an evil curse. There is no solid proof that Manawaydan was a sea god. He was also depicted as one of King Arthur's knights in some Arthurian legends.

Working with the Deities and Attracting Them into Your Life

The deities are as relevant today as they were in the past. They are prominent spiritual figures, and their tales have significantly impacted the modern-day world (more on that later). Working with them and attracting their energy into your life can help you enhance your spiritual practice. Here are some ways you can connect with each Welsh Celtic deity; you may wish to place important items on the altar:

- **Arawn**

  Put aside some time on the Winter Solstice when the night is at its longest. Arawn's energy is likely to attract dog owners or those who like to hunt.

- **Mabon**

  Mabon should be especially honored when the day and night are balanced on the Autumn Equinox.

- **Manawydan**

To honor Manawydan, remember that he helped to secure Bran's head and was closely related to King Arthur. Find items that can represent either or both of those.

- **Rhiannon**

You can hang illustrations of birds and horses near your altar and also incorporate her colors: green, purple, and white.

- **Aeronwen**

The Welsh goddess of war appreciates items of battle; you might place a small knife or another weapon on the altar. Black is a color to focus on. You can also incorporate the number 3 into your altar.

- **Arianrhod**

Worship the lunar goddess Arianrhod on the Full moon. You can hang pictures or paintings of the moon around your altar or in your home to honor her.

- **Branwen**

Branwen encourages marriage filled with love – and love in general. You can place photos of yourself and your loved ones, flowers (pertaining to love and not death or sadness), and a mirror (to reflect your happy emotions and beauty).

- **Cerridwen**

If you want a significant attraction of Cerridwen's energy, you must use a cauldron. Make sure to dedicate this cauldron to her, and never use it unless you're working with her energy.

- **Modron**

Honor this god on the Autumnal Equinox. The deity loves apples and can be asked for help with problems related to motherhood.

The Impact of the Mabinogi and Welsh Mythology

To this day, mythology plays a huge role in Welsh history and culture. The national flag of Wales even has an image of a red dragon, Y Ddraig Goch, considered the mythological creature of Wales.

As you probably know by now, *The Mabinogi* is considered the most prominent source of folktales and myths. It encompasses a total of 11 tales dating back to the Middle Ages. The Mabinogi's author is anonymous, but the tales have been passed on from one generation to the other. Since storytelling is an oral tradition, each teller or group added their own take on the tales until they were finally written in the Middle Welsh language and kept in the *White Book of Rhydderch* between 1300 and 1325. The myths were also written between 1375 and 1410 in *The Red Book of Hergest*.

These stories were about the troubles and adversities of Welsh royal families, plagues, a Roman emperor, voyages, white horses, and mystical creatures. However, these books weren't translated into English until the 19th century. A woman from Lincolnshire developed an interest in the Welsh language and translated the stories to English. Not long after, they made it across Europe and the rest of the world.

Lady Charlotte Guest, the wife of the Dowlais Ironworks' owner, gathered the tales and titled them *The Mabinogion*. However, many people mistakenly thought this title was the plural of the word *Mabinogi*. A Cardiff University emeritus professor, Sioned Davies, translated the Mabinogion into English. She incorporated it into the Oxford World Classics and continued to study and teach it for the majority of her life.

The Mabingoni and the *Mabingonion* were by different authors and were created in different periods, even though they were all collected by Lade Charlotte Guest on a known date. As we discussed, The Four Branches of the Mabingoni encompasses the structure and overtones of Celtic mythology, including imagery and concepts like white horses, shapeshifting, and other greater worlds.

The Four Branches include the stories of Pwyll, Prince of Dyfed, Branwen, daughter of Llŷr, Manawydan, son of Llŷr, and Math, Son of Mathonwy. These, along with the other seven tales, were all collected in *The Mabinogion* by Lady Charlotte Guest. The Mabinogion, especially *The Four Branches of the Mabingoni,* significantly influenced Welsh culture and literature. Think of them as the Chaucer and Shakespeare of English literature. Many elements of these tales are also seen in internationally significant pieces, like *Star Wars* and the works of *Doctor Who and JK Rowling.*

The Four Branches of the Mabingoni are considered more inspirational than the Arthurian legend because they are more relatable to the modern-day world because they have prominent themes like friendship. Their characters are more relevant to the present day.

The works have also been translated into numerous languages, including Hungarian, German, and French. Lady Guest's initial translation allowed the world to see the grandeur of *The Mabinogion.* It has greatly impacted the cultural landscape and filmmakers, writers, musicians, and artists ever since. Some illustrators like Alan Lee and Margaret Jones took an interest in illustrating the tales, while artists like Iwan Bala completed paintings inspired by the tales. Along with other writers, Jenny Nimmo was also deeply inspired by *The Mabinogion.* The impact of the tales could be seen in works like *The Magician Trilogy and The Snow Spider.* A Welsh national opera named The Sacrifice was also based on *The Second Branch of the Mabinogi.* Renowned writers like Gwyneth Lewis, Owen Sheers, Russell Celyn Jones, and Fflur Dafydd also worked on a modern re-telling of the tales by Seren Books, which was among the latest adaptations.

There are numerous Welsh gods and goddesses with remarkable tales. Calling on them as a part of your spiritual practice can enrich your experience. Their tales have influenced the cultural landscape and impacted the works of numerous filmmakers, writers, musicians, and artists. Mythology is incredibly important because it has been a pure form of storytelling and a source of entertainment and education since the beginning of mankind. We all love to listen and tell good stories – mythology or not.

Chapter 7: Paganism and Druidry Today

Given the proliferation of monotheistic religions, followed by widespread secularism in most societies, one would be forgiven for believing that paganism and Druidism went the way of other ancient practices and beliefs, forever disappearing into the ether. However, it's hard to completely eliminate religions that have lasted for longer than two millennia. Therefore, paganism and Druidry are still with us today and have taken root in their modern incarnations in various countries, specifically the west. It hasn't disappeared. On the contrary, many of the central beliefs and traditions have permeated the culture that many may not fully realize where this lore originated.

Simultaneously, there has been a steady revival of paganism and the Druidry for a few decades, with new followers adopting these ancient practices in droves. While followers remain part of a fairly niche religious movement, the numbers are growing. The exact numbers and stats aren't readily available, but given the growing market for books on the subject and stores devoted to this genre' of magic, it is easy to conclude its popularity is on the rise. Furthermore, as previously mentioned, the ways of the Druids and pagans are diffused throughout the culture and have never entirely disappeared. This chapter will devote time to understanding how paganism and Druidism take shape today.

More than Just a Holiday

Many of our most popular holidays these days, or the specific ways they're celebrated, possess pagan roots. One famous example is Christmas. Of course, the intention of this holiday is to celebrate the birth of Christ, which is about as far as you can be from the pagan or Druid beliefs. However, there is a great deal of historical evidence that the Catholic Church remade the pagan winter solstice to entice people into Christianity, and the traditions of Judeo-Christians and pagans have been woven into the holiday. The exact date of Jesus' birth is unknown, and there is no evidence in the Christian Bible. December

25th is a random date until you realize it most likely coincided with many festivities the pagans performed to celebrate the winter solstice. It was a clever intervention on the church's part to gently wean pagans off their religious practices and render the newer religion more relatable and palatable.

Next, of course, is Halloween. Unlike Christmas or the winter solstice, Halloween has managed to retain much of its original character. So much so that many strident believers in the major monotheistic religions will say celebrating Halloween is evil and has no place in the daily life of Christians or others. Halloween, or All Hallows Eve, originates from the pagan holiday of Samhain that occurs on October 31st, and is a time to honor the dead. It's also traditionally considered a spiritually discombobulating day wherein the boundary between our world and the next is at its weakest and most porous. This holiday and much of its attendant traditions are so powerful that non-pagans continue to celebrate it for thousands of years. Its popularity has continued to grow with time on a global scale, keeping a vital element of pagan religion alive and well.

Of course, Easter is another excellent example of a holiday with distinct pagan roots taken over to better accommodate the sensibilities of a growing Christian populace and the powerful church. Easter is a more modern incarnation of the spring solstice, and everything from the image of the Easter bunny to the act of finding eggs in a forest possesses deep roots in a pagan culture.

Aside from the major holidays, there are tons of traditions and mundane superstitions we've held onto for thousands of years, even though they derive from the beliefs of pagans and Druids. For example, our singular obsession with cats and all they symbolize have roots in pagan beliefs, as does knocking on wood to ward off bad luck or wearing flower crowns at a spring music festival. These are all things with pagan roots and sacred beliefs with a long history that continues with us today.

Neopaganism

Many religious practices of the pagans, Druids, and other polytheistic religions have been revived in the past few years. This "revival" of sorts has been referred to as neopaganism, is on the rise, and presents one key way paganism and Druidry have remained with us. At the same time, simply referring to these various trends in spirituality as neopaganism fails to recognize different nuances.

Neopaganism sets itself apart from these different practices in that it strives to revive authentic rituals of ancient culture, sometimes in seemingly strange or deliberately restorative ways. These days, most individuals with romantic feelings towards nature or who possess deep ecological concerns will turn to neopaganism and all the attendant dramatic, vibrant rituals as the very personification of nature and life. The pagan holy days and general motifs are sources of inspiration for neopagans and ensure that elements central to the lives of pagans and Druids survive.

Much of neopaganism has its roots in the Romanticism 19th century movement. Even organizations like the British Order of Druids originate from that, even though they claim to have an older, ancient lineage. Furthermore, instead of focusing solely on the customs of the pagans of Western Europe, neopagans are known to adopt other traditions, like Ancient Egypt or polytheistic African religions. This underscores another way of saying neopaganism is an extension of ancient pagan traditions is a bit of an oversimplification. Nonetheless, it proves that some central practices remain alive and well today through this revival of the ancient spiritual practices.

Neopaganism, as practiced these days, also has a dark side. There are quite a few neopagan groups associated with extreme nationalism, influenced by individuals such as Hitler, who deeply believed in a few pagan rituals representing white supremacy. Even before World War II, certain neopagan groups expressed anti-Semitic and deeply racist sentiments, although, arguably, much of contemporary neopaganism is a by-product of the freewheeling 1960s. So, the vast majority of neopagans do not entirely espouse negative beliefs but are more likely influenced by psychiatrist Carl Jung and writer Robert Graves. They loved nature and were not at all interested in *nationalism* of any kind.

Many neopagans these days would like to clarify that they are not to be confused with Wiccans. It is easy to conflate both spiritual practices since these groups honor old traditions in equal measures, but their attitudes and beliefs vary considerably. Wicca is one form of contemporary witchcraft, and witchcraft is only one pillar of paganism. Therefore, Wicca is a tradition of the pagan culture and was originally founded by Gerald Gardner in the 1950s – but it is not by any means the same as paganism. This will be further explained in the next section.

Wicca and the Rule of Three

"An it harm none, do what thou wilt." Does this adage sound familiar? If so, then you're more up to speed on the understanding of contemporary Wicca than you think. This saying is part of the Wiccan Rede, which, in essence, is a statement that provides the key moral system in the Wiccan religion. While other neopagans may identify with the rede, it primarily forms the spine of modern Wicca and other related witchcraft-based faiths.

The word "rede" means "advice" or "counsel," which makes sense when you think of the implications behind this verse. It is meant to guide the modern witch to use their magic without hurting others.

At this point, you're probably wondering how Wiccans define themselves and view their relationship to ancient paganism and Druidry. While they are a distinct religion and have their own set of practices and principles, Wiccans take the ancient rituals and prayers of pagans seriously. They have incorporated many facets of that belief system into their own. However, its origins are very modern, and the way it has entered the mainstream is fairly specific to its history.

As we know it today, Wicca seems to be either a hyper-feminine, new age-y religion with legions of female followers or something more akin to the scary teens featured in the cult 1990s film The Craft. Of course, Wicca is nothing like these common stereotypes, even though they bear some familiarity. The religion was developed in England during the first half of the 20th century and introduced to the public in 1954 by Gerald Gardner, who, ironically, was a retired British civil servant. Despite his buttoned-up occupation during the day, Gardner cultivated a deep appreciation for paganism and various ancient rituals, drawing inspiration from their theological structures and practices to create his 20th-century spin on the religion.

Because Wicca does not possess a central figure of authority, nor does it believe in centralized places of worship like a church or synagogue, there has been considerable disagreement on what constitutes Wicca. Its roots have consistently been up for debate, for better or for worse, making it difficult for many people to fully appreciate just how unique this religion is.

In terms of theology, Wicca is a purely duo-theistic religion, worshiping a goddess and a god. These higher beings are typically viewed as the Triple goddess and the Horned god. They each have specific divine aspects, and these characteristics have their roots in diverse pagan deities throughout history. For this reason, they are sometimes referred to as the Great Goddess or the Great Horned god. The word "great" denotes that the deity contains other deities within their nature. It's a nesting egg of sorts, and this distinction is important for Wiccans. It also indicates that Wicca was created as a patchwork adaptation of older elements; many were taken from pre-existing religions or pagan movements previously disconnected from one another.

While Gardner worked to formulate this religion, and it started practicing in the first half of the 20th century, it is clear from his writings that he never intended it to be a strict revival of Druidry or paganism. Rather, Wicca is a contemporary religion that prioritizes witchcraft and provides a fairly contemporary spin on many pagan precepts. While Wiccans celebrate the changes in season, and the most important holidays are the Winter Solstice or Spring Solstice, they diverge from other neopagans through a specific form of worship and newly written prayers or rituals. In general, Wiccans don't pretend to revive exact replicas of ancient traditions and festivities. Instead, they present paganism through the prism of 20th Century concerns and mores.

However, one belief that is shared among Wiccans, neopagans, and other occultists is the Rule of Three. This dictates that any energy a person puts out into the world, whether positive or negative, will be returned threefold to that person. Think of it as a Western version of beliefs like karma. Some practitioners believe this law is too strict and uphold a slight variation where the comeback would be less than threefold, but the general idea is easily understood.

Most occultists have stated in their research that the Rule of Three presents a direct "reward or punishment tied to one's actions, particularly when working magic." Wiccans, neopagans, Druids, and other occultists widely disagree on how to interpret such a tenet. Some historians have neglected the extent to which different groups believe in this adage. While the Rule of Three can be accurately ascertained to represent one of the central beliefs carried on by pagans throughout the centuries, not all Wiccans believe it. By that same token, because not all neopagans practice witchcraft, they may not find much truth in this rule.

Whether more experienced or new to the faith, Wiccans sometimes debate the Rule of Three and view it as an over-interpretation of the Wiccan Rede. Others still debate the extent to its representative of ancient beliefs and whether it is a more modern idea inspired primarily by Christian morality. On the other hand, Wiccans who firmly believe in this law often turn to a key piece of Wiccan liturgy Gerald Gardner initially printed in the influential 1949 novel, *High Magic's Aid.* All in all, The Rule of Three is not such an outlier for ancient beliefs, and different iterations of this basic idea exist throughout the world, either as the concept of karma, widely believed among Dharmic religion followers, or the more modern "Golden Rule."

According to recorded history, The Rule of Three was mentioned extensively by the famed witch Raymond Buckland who practically wrote the modern text on the Wiccan religion after Gardner officiated the spiritual practice. Prior to Buckland's innovation, the very idea of reciprocal ethics in Wicca was nebulous, ill-defined, and difficult to nail down. Any consequences of magical practice, whether negative or positive, were assigned a general understanding of karma and nothing more. There is some skepticism within the Wiccan community about applying The Rule of Three to their practice since Buckland expounded on the idea in 1968 – hardly an "ancient" date. Later, The Rule of Three became the basis of *The Wiccan Rede*, published by Lady Gwen Thompson in 1975.

The debates on The Rule of Three's exact application – and the Wiccan Rede, for that matter – are endless. However, the heart of these ideas is shared among many neopagans and others identifying as members of an occult. The core of this spiritual practice is seen as a vivid, thorough line from ancient beliefs to the contemporary moment, rendered tangible through writing and drafting poetry.

Celtic Paganism

One group of people with a tremendous influence in maintaining and shaping the contemporary understanding of paganism and Druidry today is Celtic paganism. This last iteration is very different from those discussed above, primarily because it adheres more formally to a polytheistic reconstruction of Celtic neopaganism. It emphasizes historical accuracy instead of romanticizing myths or rituals. Followers also emphasize specific theological concerns of Druidry in a more authentic effort to revive the pre-Christian Celtic way of life. These efforts are fairly modern, having originated in the writings of amateur scholars and members of neopagan communities in the mid-1980s, who were tired of how diluted some of these ancient beliefs came to be. While this movement is far from being a monolith and has several subgroups and denominations, they are united in a belief that the specific cultural context of the Celts must be upheld.

Celtic pagans believe ancient rituals need to be divorced from Christian incarnations that came later. Folklore, myths, and legends are excellent ways to introduce people to ancient ways without misinterpreting or peppering them with too many contemporary interpretations. They strongly believe in the beauty of these ancient traditions and that their rich legacies must be preserved for future generations. A thorough line that runs throughout these conversations among Celtic pagans is the sense of urgency and fear that much of the Celts' ancient culture and unique traditions are at risk of disappearing forever. Therefore, this sense permeates all their work and their specific paganism practice.

The movement had its origins in the 1980s but became a genuine phenomenon in the last thirty years, given the proliferation of the internet and the attendant online forums allowing free and open discussion among pagans. They established that an important part of their spiritual practice is advocating for the protection of Celtic archeological and sacred sites. This is why construction projects like the potential destruction of the Hill of Tara in Ireland a few years ago made the news. Historians, archivists, and passionate Celtic pagans joined forces to organize and protest the construction and worked hard to establish the site as a historical landmark worthy of protection by the state.

Celtic pagans don't have many centralizing texts of their own, and they acknowledge that the structure of their belief system may be perceived as a bit spotty given the obvious absence. While they work hard to revive these religious practices and the beliefs of ancient Celtic people as accurately as possible, they will always forthrightly acknowledge some aspects are reconstructions. They cannot verify the historical accuracy of some of the rituals and traditions they work hard to revive. Still, they take cultural survival seriously, and rigorous study is an important part of their practice. They augment their beliefs with scholars' and archeologists' work and downplay the importance of stories or myths if they do not have evidence – regardless of whether or not they are verifiable by historians.

The groups mentioned throughout this chapter work hard to preserve and maintain the legacy of pagans and Druids in their distinct ways. While there are many differences, they are joined by the desire to pay homage to the ancient ways and keep an important part of cultural history alive and thriving.

Chapter 8: Magickal Tools and How to Use Them

The word "magick" is not just a trendy spelling for the word magic, nor is it a spelling associated with pagans or Druidry. Magick is specific magic used for good. Generally, magic is associated with negativity causing harm to others or altering things for personal gain. Magick is about helping others through using different tools, spells, and skills associated with or connected to the spiritual realm. This chapter will explore the various magickal tools and how they're used in Wiccan and Pagan traditions. We'll also discuss the relationship between magick and Paganism and delve deep into the process of magical practice. Upon reading this chapter, you'll learn about the significance of animals in Irish pagan magical practices. Finally, you'll find out about the role that crystals play in magic and how you can select one that suits your needs.

Magical Tools

When people first develop an interest in any form of Paganism, they are quick to purchase all sorts of magical tools that they can get their hands on. Many people fail to realize that each tool comes with a significant and specific purpose; this is why you need to know which tools and ritual items to buy and what to use them for. It's worth noting that many of these items are not common across all traditions, and those that are aren't always used in the same way.

- ● Altar

    This book dedicates an entire chapter to altars and setting them up to incorporate them into your spiritual practice, which signifies their importance in the pagan practice. Altars play an important role in ritual and celebration. In most religions and mythologies, altars are used to honor gods, perform rituals, and offer sacrifice. This does not need to be a crafted altar; an altar at home is as simple as a small table with your tools and offerings. You can change the theme, decorations, and items to match the season you're celebrating. You can also dedicate an altar to the deity you worship by including their images, their associated colors, symbols, etc. Some people also have more than one altar in their homes. Ancestral altars are very common. They include ashes, photos, or heirlooms from family members who have passed on. Having a nature altar is not an uncommon practice either. Many people use it to showcase interesting and rare items that they collect, such as unique rocks, alluring seashells, and even patterned pieces of wood. If you have children you wish to introduce to the concept of spirituality and religious practices, you can have them help you set up the altar or even have them create their own in their rooms.

- **Athame**

An athame is a double-edged dagger that you can make your own or purchase ready-made. This tool can be as simple or as embellished and personified as you wish. Many pagan rituals include the use of this tool to direct energy. The athame is mostly used when casting a circle. It is also used as an alternative for wands. This tool is not meant to be used to cut actual items. Creating your own athame can be a very fun DIY project. The process is as simple or as complicated as your metalworking skill level. This is why you should make sure to find online instructions that suit your abilities.

- **Besom**

Witches' brooms are not used for flying – they are used to help cleanse a room. A traditional broom is known as a Besom. This tool is used to clean a place by sweeping it before a ritual. When we sweep a room with a Besom, we are removing the negative energies that reside in the room – a practice that is essential if you are to perform a ceremony or a ritual in the room. The Besom is associated with the element Water because it serves as a purifier. Many pagans have a wide array of brooms since they're very easy to make. Brooms can be crafted from almost any material, but if you are making a traditional Besom, birch is used for the brush and oak or ash for the staff.

- **Bell**

Bells are common in many ceremonies, both religious and non-religious. Spirits are driven away by certain noises, and the act of ringing a bell in a room or larger area can drive away any evil or negative spirits in a room. This is due to the loudness of a bell and the frequency at which the bell rings. The vibrations move through a room and help to clear it. You can find other instruments to ward off evil spirits as long as there is a vibrational quality. While you can ring bells before performing a ritual or ceremony, you should try to bookend the ceremony by ringing the bell at the beginning and the end.

- **Candles**

Candles are one of the most commonly used tools in Pagan practices and rituals. Not only is it used to represent the element of Fire and as a symbol of various deities, like Badb and Brigid, candles are usually also an element of spell workings. This is because it is suggested that candles can absorb an individual's personal energy. As the candle burns, it releases this unwanted energy. You may be surprised to learn that it is customary to leave the candle burning for a set number of days as part of the spell in some traditions. Many people believe that creating your own candle makes it a lot more powerful than ready-made ones. This is why they prefer making their own candles. Others, however, believe that it is the intention that purely matters. They focus on the inter that they put into the spell rather than pay much attention to where the candle came from or how it was made. Most traditions, however, focus on the colors of the candle, as it is an important aspect when it comes to candle magic.

- **Pentacle**

The pentacle is used in May pagan practices, but don't confuse the pentacle with the pentagram – they sound very alike, but they are very different. A pentagram is a five-pointed star, while a pentacle is a flat slab with symbols carved into it. People incorporate this tool into ceremonial magic and use it as a protective talisman. Most Wiccan and Pagan traditions also view the pentacle as a symbol of the element of Earth. Pagans and Wiccans often place this tool on their altars to hold the items they will consecrate as part of a ritual. Pentacles can be easily made (all you need is a slab of sanded wood and a wood-burning kit) or purchased from a specialized store.

- **Book of Shadows – BOS**

The Book of Shadows should include all the significant magical information that belongs to its owner's tradition and spiritual practice. Despite what movies and novels have led us to believe, there is not just one book of shadows. The BOS is supposed to be personal and unique to its owner, as it serves as a notebook of all the information they believe is crucial. This book can contain rituals, spells, the rules of magic and relevant information, correspondent charts, lore and myths, tales about the deities, invocations, and more. Many pagans decide to pass on this book from one generation to the other. However, if you don't have a BOS passed down from your great-great-grandmother, you can make one yourself. While this will take a lot of effort to put together, you should enjoy the process as much as you can because it's very personal. Take the time to think about what you feel belongs in this book. Creating your own BOS can strengthen your spirituality and make you feel even more connected to your tradition.

- **Cauldron**

Cauldrons, like chalices, are very common tools in goddess-oriented beliefs and traditions. Cauldrons are very feminine and are shaped like a womb. It is symbolic of the vessel of life. Because they are vessels, cauldrons are connected to the element Water, and they can be used in many rituals and celebrations. Use them also in any celebrations where knowledge is sought. They are vessels of water, but they are also vessels for other things, such as knowledge and inspiration. For instance, you can use it to present offerings or burn candles and incense. Many goddesses of several traditions can also be represented through the cauldron. You can also use the tool to blend herbs and use them for magical purposes. Many people use cauldrons for moonlight scrying after filling them up with water. If you commonly use cauldrons for cooking purposes, make sure to dedicate a separate one for your magical practices. Many magical practices will make your cauldron no longer suitable for cooking.

- **Chalices**

As we just mentioned, the chalice is often strongly associated with female deities and archetypes. It is also a feminine symbol that is symbolic of the womb and is representative of the Water element. The chalice is often used alongside the athame in some practices. When re-enacting the Great Rite, symbolically, this combination is representative of the Divine Feminine. You can use a chalice of any material, like pewter and silver, on your altar. You can also use it to provide offerings for your deity. However, if you're offering wine, you should be mindful of untreated metals. Ceramic chalices are now more popularly used and are easy to get ahold of. Many individuals use chalices of different materials depending on the ritual they're conducting.

- **Divination Tools**

There are numerous divination tools and methods that you can choose from to enrich your magical and spiritual practice. Many people like to experiment with different types of divination tools rather than stick to one method. However, it's normal to feel most comfortable using a particular divination tool or feel that you're a naturally gifted area. Some methods may simply not work out for you. For instance, you may be able to grasp a natural understanding of tarot and oracle cards but feel completely lost when it comes to the Ogham staves, and that's okay. Some examples of common divination tools are:

- Numerology

- Tarot cards

- I ching coins and books

- Pendulums

- Essential oils

- Crystals

- Signs and signals

- Stream-of-consciousness writing

- The practice of opening books on random pages to receive messages

- Animal messages

- **Crystals**

You can select from and incorporate countless stones into your healing and spiritual practices. The stones that you choose to work with should depend on your intentions. This is why you should make sure to select ones based on their associations and characteristics rather than their aesthetic appeal. We will delve deeper into that topic and cover the uses and attributes of multiple crystals later throughout the chapter. Birthstones also work well in magical practices. Make sure to cleanse your crystal or gemstone before your first use.

- **Ritual Robe**

If you want to give your rituals a more special feel, you can wear a robe during the process. Ritual robes are very easy to make and can be worn in any color and style, depending on what your tradition or practice calls for. Many people don't care much about what they're wearing to perform their rituals. After all, it's the intent that matters. However, wearing a robe is significant for others because they think of it as a way to separate their spiritual practices from the mundane activities of daily life. Putting the robe on signifies stepping into a spiritual mindset or making your way from the physical realm to the magical realm.

- **Wand**

You can purchase a wand from a specialized store or make one that's as simple or as lavish and decorative as you wish. When we think of magic, a picture of a want immediately comes to mind. As stereotypical as this sounds, the wand is among the most popular and commonly used magical tools in the world of Wicca and Paganism. Wands are created to fulfill a wide array of magical purposes, including directing energy throughout rituals. Wands represent power, valor, and of course, masculine energy (it is a phallic symbol, after all). Wands are used in the air, and so they are connected to that element. Staffs can be seen as a type of wand, but they are connected to fire, and that is an important distinction depending on what you are trying to achieve. You can use the wand to invoke a deity or consecrate a sacred area. We associate wands closely with wood (and you might also think about items or ingredients infused into the wood), but wood is not the only material that can be used. Almost any material can be used, and the user is more important than the object. Many practitioners have a wide collection of wands, especially those who don't use athames.

- **Magic Staff**

Like the athame and wands, the staff can be used for the purpose of energy direction, according to some traditions. Many Wiccans and Pagans incorporate the use of magical staff into their ceremonies, rituals, and spiritual activities. Even though it's not a vital magical tool, it can be of great help, considering that it's linked to authority and power. Some of them even believe that these divine figures are the only ones allowed to carry this tool. On the other hand, other traditions permit all practitioners to use the staff. Staffs are more closely associated with male energy and fire, but they can be used in place of wands and can represent air at times too. Like many of the tools we mentioned above, you can make your own staff instead of purchasing one.

Paganism and Magick

The idea of spirituality and magick is very closely related to Pagan beliefs. Even though different pagan groups have varying religious perspectives, the underlying framework that serves as the metaphysical phenomena basis and the magical activities is relatively similar. There are a few core tenants of this philosophy. The first aspect is the involvement of animals in the idea of god and the idea of magic. Secondly, the incorporation of various natural elements as spirits: the spirits of fire, water, air, and earth. Thirdly, the concept of God is not limited to one god but rather there is a god and goddess, and in some cases, there are multiple goddesses. Lastly, the spiritual or magical practices performed can be done individually or in a group.

The magical practices performed by pagans are used for a range of purposes. The most common are:

- To induct someone into the coven or group

- As a celebration of the season

- To honor the deity

- To get attuned with nature

- To attain self-realization

- For magical healing

The process of magical practice is split into three parts which are sometimes not that easy to identify. First is the separation phase, the second is a testing phase, and lastly, reintegration.

Separation

The first phase is the separation phase. The aim is to differentiate between the physical world and the spiritual world. Unlike most other religions, pagans do not have a dedicated place of worship like a church or a temple. Instead, the sacred place of worship is created wherever they feel like worshiping, and it is done whenever they wish to worship. The most common way is through a process known as "casting the circle."

It is physically demarcating a space, usually in the form of a circle, using things like salt, rocks, or candles, and consecrating the space by invoking the spiritual entities and deities. In some cases, casting the circle is done with magical and holy tools like a wand or a ritual knife. The practitioners ask these deities to bless the space they have created and invite the deity to the space to bless it with their presence, and also ask the deity to assist in the practices they will exercise in that space. Creating a holy space is common among all pagan religions. Mainly, people create this space in their home, but for some festivals, they create this outside where they can also make a fire to assist with the process. This sacred space is an area at the border of the physical and the spiritual world while not being part of either.

Testing

The second part of the process is the activity that takes place within the circle. It is known as the testing phase as it "tests" the strength of the circle. The practices that take place within the circle can vary a lot depending on the aim of the exercise. However, all practices have three distinct parts. The first part is to raise the energy level or create the energy needed. The second step is to give that energy a purpose and charge it to the desired level. The final step is to focus and direct this energy toward the recipient.

The different practices that happen in the circle are all dependent on the desired outcome and what is appropriate for that particular event. For instance, the festival of Beltane is highlighted by fire, and fertility is celebrated. However, the spirit of the festival is also celebrated metaphorically – writing down your desires and casting them into the fire, so they are delivered to the universe and the gods. Or the process of planting seeds into pots of soil in the sacred space to represent planting seeds of joy and happiness within ourselves. Then there are customized spells used for particular things like attracting money into one's life, enhancing love in a relationship, or healing from a physical or emotional injury. For instance, the practitioner will use relevant stones and tools to enhance love and induce positive energy.

Reintegration

This is the final step of the process. When the energy is raised, the interactions with the entities and the entire process of creating desired outcomes are directed to the person it is meant for. At the same time, this is also the process where the practitioner and the subject ground themselves and "seal" the portal they opened to connect to the spiritual realm. This final process is essential to ensure the energy that has been transferred to the recipient of the energy given to the tools used during the divination process is safely stored in them.

Grounding can be done in two ways. The first and most common way is through visualization. The practitioner and the subject visualize themselves becoming part of the earth and reconnecting with the physical world. People who practice tree magic often visualize they are growing roots into the earth like a tree grows roots and gets a stronger grip on the earth. It also acts as a way to discard the excess energy as the earth soaks up the excess energy dissipated through the roots.

The second way is to consume "blessed" food and drink that is believed to return a person to their normal state. Generally, this includes wine and cake, but some people also prefer other drinks like a lager or non-alcoholic juice. Cakes can be of any kind, and some people prefer to have a savory baked item. This is followed by dismantling the circle and thanking the entities that were there to help in the process.

Animals and Magic

Animals also have a special place in Irish Paganism. In some cases, they are used metaphorically, and, in other cases, they have a physical presence in the practices. One of the most common animal concepts in Paganism is the idea of the power animal. Also known as the Totem animal or spirit animal, it is when a person identifies with a certain animal as their spirit guardian. Similar to how people find spirit guardians from the spiritual realm that are other entities, totem animals take the form of an animal and play the same role. Another concept that resonated with spirit animals is the concept of "Familiars." An animal familiar is identified as an animal a person has a special bond with or feels a strong connection with. Familiars are physical animals existing in the real world but have a spirit belonging to the spiritual world. The person connects with them at a much deeper level.

Animal parts are used in various rituals and in the casting spell process. Usually, things like snake skins, a goat's jaw, a stag's antlers, or even a big cat's fur can be used in spiritual practices. Tools are often made from these items, such as knife handles made from the bones of an animal, or a shawl made from an animal's hide. In other cases, parts of the animal are used directly in the magic process, a snake's skin. Also, most of these items are collected rather than the animal being hunted down just for a specific part. These can be collected from animals used as an offering to the gods, animals that have died naturally, or things that animals leave naturally, shed skin, or broken antlers.

Birds also have a very important place in magic. Some are seen as a sign of bad news, danger, or even the onset of a natural disaster. Others are considered messengers delivering a message from the spiritual world. The challenge is to properly decipher what they are saying and use that knowledge for its intended purpose. Among the birds, the owl is one of the most important. The owl has a special place in many cultures, but it is associated with the goddess Athena in Paganism. It symbolizes the goddesses' wisdom and knowledge.

Crystals and Magic

It is unnecessary to have accessories like herbs, wands, and crystals when practicing magic. However, these assets can improve your magic's effectiveness tremendously. If there was one thing you could invest in, or you are starting to dabble with magic accessories and want something to make a tangible impact on your practices, it has to be crystals. Here are some of the best crystals to consider and their benefits.

• Clear Quartz

Of all the thousands of different crystals available, the clear quartz should be your choice if you had to choose just a single one. It is a neutral stone and can be used for practically anything, especially if you get a clear quartz stone with a pointed tip. This quartz can be a very powerful tool. The great thing about clear quartz is that it works extremely well with other accessories. It can amplify the power of other tools you are using. So, whether you have other stones, herbs, or anything else to use, it will get amplified using clear quartz. You can use this stone for meditation, therapy, magic, and even protection.

• Citrine

Citrine is part of the quartz family, and just like clear quartz, it is a very powerful crystal. However, this stone has a misty orange and sometimes yellow shade to it and is particularly efficient for cleansing and other healing processes. It is a stone with the ability to soak up energy in its surroundings, so it is fantastic for cleansing a space, your other stones, and magick tools, and even clearing out negative influences from your home. Other than cleansing, this stone is used to enhance your psychic ability, making it a great stone to have when you are meditating or things like astral travel.

• Rose Quartz

The quartz stone is a potent crystal for magic, and different variations are good for specific things. For instance, the rose quartz is extremely good for love, emotions, and even spiritual work. This is the crystal to use if you are casting spells based on emotions and, specifically, love. It's a very grounded crystal, so it can also be used to manage situations with intense emotional energy. For instance, this is the stone to use if you are trying to diffuse a matter between two people or helping a person get more clarity and peace in their mind.

• Amber

Amber is a very powerful stone if you are seeking something to offer you protection. It is often associated with the sun due to its color. However, it also has a deep relationship with the Earth. In reality, amber is not a crystal but fossilized tree sap, meaning it has spent millions of years deep underground and is a product of plants and not stone. For this reason, it has a very powerful connection to the earth and does a tremendous job as a grounding stone.

• Malachite

This is a favorite stone of the green witches largely because of its color. However, others can still use it, and it is great for meditation and even protection from danger. It is commonly associated with consciousness and is often used for things like fortune-telling and understanding at a deeper level. It is one of those stones that can be worn daily and used for dedicated practices and grounding rituals.

• Obsidian

This is another stone that is a favorite of the witches as it was also the favorite stone of the goddess of witches, Hecate. Although this stone is associated with protection and can absorb all energy forms, it is also typically used for scrying mirrors. Obsidian is a great source of energy and is known as a very powerful stone largely because of its origins. Obsidian is born out of volcanic eruptions and is, therefore, associated with fire. If you are practicing banishing magic, this stone will be very handy.

- **Tigers Eye**

Like the animal it is known for, Tigers Eye is used as a source of strength, courage, and fierceness. It is great for people wanting to improve their self-confidence and needing a boost of positive energy. It is an all-purpose stone that works exceptionally well in conjunction with other stones; white quartz will amplify its energy. It can also be paired with black obsidian to give you an incredibly holistic defense.

- **Blood Stone**

The bloodstone is named not because it is red. Instead, it is a green stone with flecks of red in it. This stone is excellent if you are working on your health or a patient's health and can also be used for protection.

- **Moonstone**

Milky white in color and ruled by the moon, this stone is excellent for everything with intuition, consciousness, dreams, and general matters of the mind. This stone can also be used in place of other stones, such as quartz, amethyst, or bloodstone.

You can easily buy these stones at your local metaphysics store or even find them at your local jewelry store. However, keep in mind that stones you find or are given to you hold more power than those you buy at a store. Also, if you have these stones as a necklace or a bracelet, you can still use them for your witchcraft.

Practicing Magick

Other than the main components of practicing magick, such as crystals or animals, other components make this possible. Whether you are casting spells or performing a spiritual cleansing, you can use different tools for better effect.

One of the most important instruments for witches practicing magick is a wand. Usually, this is made from crystals, such as quartz or ammolite, and comes in a variety of sizes and shapes. The most common shape is stick-shaped and 6 to 8 inches long with a blunt end or pointed end. The pointed wands are usually used in practices where reflexology is involved or if the practitioner wants to focus energy at a particular point. Blunt wands are commonly used in cleansing practices and in situations where the stone transfers energy to larger areas, such as a room in a house or a group of people.

As we mentioned above, altars are also essential equipment to have; they will be discussed in great detail in the next chapter. You can either have a specially-made altar designed to practice magic and other sacred practices or use a make-shift altar with any elevated table in your home. Altars are usually decorated with sacred items, such as sacred texts or objects used as symbols. What you place on your altar depends entirely on the purpose of the spell or ritual.

You should also use salt to demarcate an area for magical practices. Some people prefer to demarcate an area by digging a shallow trench around the area or using candles. Salt works particularly well as its energy is excellent for keeping unwanted forces out – and it also helps to retain all the energy within that space. You should also have some candles for your magic practice. In some cases, this is used to define the area. In other cases, fire and light are ingredients used in the process.

How You Can Get Started

Most of the things you'll need, like salt, crystals, or herbs, are items you can easily get at your local hardware or grocery store. If you are looking for something very particular and not available in your locality, you always have the option of ordering online. As Paganism, in all forms, becomes more popular and people worldwide gain interest in this philosophy, there is an increasing demand for tools and equipment. Many sellers worldwide manufacture these items, and many are accomplished witches who love to handcraft many products. Handcrafted versions can be a bit pricey, so there is no harm in getting a more economical option if you are just starting. Determine if you genuinely like it, then get a higher quality version. As a starting point, look into what you want to do and the spells you want to practice and get equipment catering to those needs. Some things, like quartz crystals, can be used for many things, so it is always a good investment. If you want to do very specific things, find out what you need and invest accordingly. Also, be sure to cleanse all your equipment after use, and refresh it before every use.

Chapter 9: Setting Up a Pagan Altar

To practice your pagan rituals, you need a special space, and you can achieve this by creating an altar. If you want to create a shrine, there are different steps you can take. This chapter outlines the significance of an Irish or Welsh pagan altar and the tips for building one. It also discusses different tools you can place on the altar and their purpose.

Significance of a Pagan Altar

A pagan altar is a sacred space where you place spiritual objects used for ritual, spells, meditation, prayers, visualizations, divination, and connecting to the deity. Pagans use this workspace, also called a shrine, to do their ritual work. An altar is a personal place where a practitioner puts different ritual items. This place is mainly used for religious spell works. If you cannot perform your rituals outside, you can create a shrine inside your home.

It is usually a raised platform or structure used for prayer or worship. The Wiccan practitioners often find several symbolic and functional items used to worship the goddess and god, say chants and prayers, and cast spells. You can also use your altar to connect with the spiritual world in various forms. You may use this platform for performing rituals, such as celebrating seasonal cycles, devotion to a deity, or rites of passage. The items you use to decorate your altar depend on your taste and preferences. Therefore, it is an excellent idea that your altar reflects your spirituality.

Your altar can be of any size or shape, and you choose the material you want. Many people believe that wood is the best medium since it comes from the earth. However, stone and metal also work well for your shrine. While there is no universal structure of the altar, it is usually believed that the left side is the goddess area. Feminine symbols like chalices, bowls, and other symbols representing goddesses and statues are placed in this area. On the other hand, the right side is meant for gods, and symbols like the wand and the athame are put here. The god statuary and his candle are also found on the right side of the altar.

The center area of the altar is known as the working space or both areas. The cauldron associated with four elements is placed in the center. You should know that Irish Pagan Practice is specifically meant for building a relationship. You can achieve this by showing up consistently at your altar and performing your religious work there.

However, it should not be hard work. Instead, it must be something that connects you with your god or goddess.

How to Make Your Pagan Altar

Before creating your altar, the first thing to do is decide whether you want something permanent or temporary. You can create a shrine to dismantle and store in a specific place. Another thing you want to consider is the location of your sacred place. You can put your altar anywhere, and other people have natural shrines outdoors. Also, take your portable altar into your garden or inside the house if you have enough space.

The good thing about creating a natural altar is it offers you a close connection with Mother Nature. If you don't have a garden, create an indoor shrine, but make sure you have a room where you can place it. Choose a corner in your bedroom where you can create a special place to perform your rituals. A bedroom is a private room, and it's easily relaxing in this room when you are alone.

When you have selected the appropriate location for your altar, make sure you determine the size and shape of the altar. You can get a chest of drawers, a table, or any movable platform. When you choose a chest, use the drawers as storage for the items you need for your rituals, like lighters, candles, and others. When practicing Irish Paganism, fire is a critical component. Whenever you perform your rites, be sure to have some form of flame, usually obtained from candles. Your space should also have a place to put your candles and ensure safety.

You must have something that represents that place to create a connection. Find something that represents a deity, don't get caught in the predicament of attempting to find a perfect statue or painting. It does not exist since the gods are shapeless and formless. Therefore, anything that helps you visualize your god can go a long way in helping you build a strong relationship.

When you design your altar, you must begin by sticking to the basics. If you want to build the shrine from scratch, make sure you get appropriate materials you can shape into desired structures. It is important to start with simple items and develop over time. Constantly develop your altar depending on your needs. Aim to create something that resonates with your intentions and get things that make sense and are special to you. Make additions to your shrine depending on your changing needs.

What Direction Should a Pagan Altar Face?

To some individuals, the direction of the altar does not matter since it can face any side. However, others consider east-facing altars since this is where the sun rises. In most traditions, the sun is associated with bringing new life or air and supporting it. As it rises, it provides the energy required to perform different things. When your altar is facing the east direction, you are appreciating its power and helping to create a strong connection with nature. The northeast is another popular direction among most Pagans since it is symbolic in their tradition.

Most rituals are believed to be associated with the North Direction since it stands for the earth. An option is to get a portable compass to set your shrine in the appropriate direction. The south direction is believed to symbolize fire, while water is for the west. The center stands for the spirit. However, you can put your altar facing any direction you believe works for you. The most important thing is that the shrine must be in a place where you can see and connect with it every day. We all have different intentions, so do not copy others. Something that works for another person might not work for you. Prioritize your needs and believe in yourself.

If your altar consists of heavy items, it will be best to build a permanent one. Other areas to consider include drawers, tree stumps, trays, and windowsills. Make sure the space is free when you decide to build an outside platform. Use your intuition to choose an ideal area for your shrine. Select corresponding items to use for your rites when the platform is immovable.

Choose the Style of Your Altar

There are many different styles of altars, so your style should be heavily influenced by Celtic Paganism and other elements like deities. For Irish and Welsh Paganism, there are specific symbols you should familiarize yourself with and know how they can help you achieve your goals. You also need to consider your practice and how the shrine will reflect your spirituality. A carefully designed altar improves the appearance of your place. If the design is an essential component to you, choose something well-crafted.

Items to Use for the Goddess

When setting up a pagan altar, it's essential to determine the items you'll use for the goddess side. The side represents the divine feminine, the moon, the right brain, unconsciousness, and nighttime. Therefore, the goddess's components differ from the ones used for the god's side. You need to get a candle with the best color you believe represents the goddess. When you practice Paganism, you should understand the significance of light. The colors for the goddess side include green, blue, purple, and silver. Do your research first to know your intentions and how you can achieve them.

Crystal balls or divination tools are other vital components you should add when you set your altar. Crystals come in various forms, and they play different roles. Therefore, when you choose crystals, make sure they align with your intentions and understand how to use them. A statue is another vital component you can add to your altar since it represents the goddess. Various forms of goddesses are available, such as Isis, the moon goddess, or totem animals. If you don't get a statue, find a drawing or image of your preferred goddess. You can also use other lunar animals as long as they suit your intentions. Other things representing feminine elements are water, like seashells, a bowl of water, a cauldron, or sea glass. Some of the earth items include brown or green-colored objects, for instance, plants, stones, bones, soil, and flowers. Depending on your intention and spiritual practice, you can get as many items as you want.

Items to Use on the God Side

Just like the goddess side, you also need to find appropriate items for the god side of your altar. The god side symbolizes the divine masculine, sun, elements of air and fire, consciousness, daytime, and the right half of the body or left brain. Some of the things you may want to put on the god side include a large candle with any color of your choice. Some colors to consider are yellow, red, orange, or gold. They should reflect your interests and other things you want to achieve.

A statue is another important item you need to add to your altar. You can use a masculine animal totem or solar imagery. The two masculine elements you may include are red or orange colors, a wand or athame, incense, candles, teeth, or claws. However, make sure you do not hurt animals to obtain these items. Also, include an oil burner or ash and feathers. Divination tools to put on the god side are also essential for your altar.

Your daily spiritual practice will determine the tools you need for your rites. Other objects special and sacred can be included on the list of items to put on the god side. The items come in different shapes and sizes, so get something that suits your altar. If your shrine is small, make sure you get portable tools to put on different sides of the gods.

Items to Put in the Center of the Altar

The center of the altar is crucial since it represents the core of your spirituality. This is the patron or matron of your deity you work with most of the time. It is important to know the deities you want to work with to get the appropriate items. Use crystals, candles, or skulls, and make sure you get something very important and powerful to represent the spirit element. These items should be white, rainbow, violet, or purple since these colors consist of great energy. Your zodiac sign should determine the candle for the center of the shrine.

If you have a pentacle representing the earth, include it on the goddess's side. A book of the shadow is another crucial item you can put in the center of the altar. An athame and wand can be placed on the god side of your shrine. If the alter is not very big, choose critical components only to declutter your space. More importantly, get things you can use, and they should also add value to your life. Always consult your paganism book of life to get the right things.

Additional Items to Put on Your Altar

The items you put on your altar mainly depend on your intentions and personal preferences. When you set your sacred place to perform your rituals, you know what you want to achieve. Therefore, feel free to include anything you think will help you achieve your desired goals. Add potpourri or herbs to your altar. You can add many different types of leaves to your place of worship, and these depend on your intentions. Additionally, include crystals since they also come in various forms. Before you get the stones, make sure you know their purpose.

Tarot or oracle cards are some items to add to your pagan altar. Cards consist of different images and designs and are usually used for meditation. You can also use them for divination if you want to know what might happen in the future. If your altar is big, add a small box you can use to store your sacred things. Spell objects are crucial since they play roles in the different forms of magic you intend to perform. Talismans and magical jewels are other items you can include when creating your altar.

Since you can use your altar for various functions, feel free to add anything divine and meaningful. Include a witches' ladder or hang a charm for energy and protection if possible. However, you need to be careful to avoid cluttering your altar with things you'll not use. If you do not know the specific function of a component, rather don't add it to your sacred space. As your needs increase, you can add the items, but do research first to get the ideal ones.

This chapter has discussed different elements to consider when setting up a Pagan Altar. You should know that everyone has a different approach when creating your sacred space for rituals. Depending on your intentions and needs, you can use any method with which you are comfortable. Make sure you put appropriate items in this sacred space since you'll need them for rituals, spells, meditation, prayers, divination, and connecting to deities. All these components should be in the right place before you begin your rites.

Chapter 10: Simple Pagan Spells and Rituals

Pagans use different rituals and ceremonies to celebrate or commemorate many aspects of life. This chapter highlights the simple pagan spells and rituals you can try if you are a practitioner. It also provides step-by-step instructions and ingredients for each recipe. Some common rituals and spells are meant for love, protection, luck, abundance, and others.

Bealtaine Rituals

In Celtic tradition, every year consists of two halves, one representing darkness and the other light. The end of the dark season heralds the coming of the light half of the year and is accompanied by celebrations known as Bealtaine. It was the most important and biggest festival on May 1ˢᵗ and is celebrated in Ireland and Scotland. Celebrating Bealtaine involves many rituals, and most include fire. During this period, supernatural beings were believed to be active, and their powers could freely pass to the mortal world.

These celebrations were meant to remind the farmers of when to sow and when to reap during the ancient period. In other words, Bealtaine festivals marked significant calendar events to mark the return of light. These celebrations were accompanied by several rituals explained below.

Fire Rituals

Fire played a critical role in these Bealtaine rituals since it symbolized the return of the sun after winter. Fire is also believed to have sympathetic magic that could enhance the growth of crops and animals. Smoke protects, and a bonfire means lots of smoke. Fire is also the great protector and provider, and the ashes have protective powers imbued in them. This is why dancing around a fire has been so prevalent in many cultures throughout history. Humans sometimes jumped over the flames.

Household fires were lit using the flames obtained from the central bonfire. In some instances, animal blood was used as a sacrifice to the gods. Bonfires were also markers for important events of the year, like the driving out of animals to pasture, and they would be a part of the celebration at these events. There were special places where the major celebrations were held every year, and the rituals were performed to protect animals, people, and crops. They were also meant to encourage growth.

Fires on the hearths inside homes were not supposed to go outside since it was believed they would carry the luck away. The fires were put out during May celebrations and rekindled using the flames from the main bonfire. From then, the fires were not allowed to go out. During this period, when the ritual was performed, people were urged to refuse requests, avoid strangers, and offer to share anything. The fire ritual was specifically meant to guard personal fortunes and other belongings. The link between the mortals and immortals was very close, so issues like death or injury were not expected.

Water and Flower Rituals

Water obtained from local wells was believed to be highly potent, and the flowers around these holy fountains were also said to be restorative. The dew on the grass on May Day was also thought to provide a cure for the entire year. According to the practitioners walking in the dew or using it to wash your face offered curative powers. Flowers were collected during the celebrations and used to decorate altars and other sacred places. Yellow flowers can ward off evil spirits, who are said to dislike the bright color. It could also be that yellow flowers contain the powers and spirit of deities, and evil spirits are repelled by such power.

Good Luck Rituals and Charms

The celebrations in May are often connected to harvest and abundance, and that brings joy and happiness. The rituals were used for luck and protection against unforeseen forces. It is good that so much power comes from celebrations and rituals at this time of the year, as it is noted that between May Eve and May Day is when evil spirits are at their most powerful. Water and yellow flower were often combined to ward off these evil spirits and bring luck. Other practices were discouraged in May since they were considered unlucky. For instance, getting married in May was considered unlucky.

In Ireland, the May Tree or May Bush is decorated. Ribbons are added to bushes or trees near to your house, and whitethorn bushes are the most traditional to decorate if they can be found in close proximity. Branches, leaves, and flowers are also hung over the door to help good luck and fortune enter the house.

Love Spells

Love spells were practiced in Irish Paganism, and these were specifically meant to bring back a lost lover or make your relationship stronger. If you wanted to bring back a lost lover, you would go to a pagan practitioner, and they would ask you the name, date of birth, and the place of birth of the person you want to reconcile with. The practitioner would also ask you the same details so they could bind your details with theirs.

There were certain ingredients required for the spell. For example, love spells would not work without ingredients like sandalwood powder and Rose petals. If you want to fall in love with someone, you have first to provide all the necessary ingredients to allow the practitioner to cast the spell. The spells were targeted, emitting an energy wave in all directions. The following are some of the basic ingredients required by the spellcasters to bring back ex-lovers.

- **Pink candles** represent your return to the lover and should be burned as long as possible before the spell is broken off.

- **Element of fire**: Fire is an essential component in a love spell since it represents passion and destruction. It would destroy the negative feelings that might have destroyed the relationship.

- **Flower herbs and petals**: You increase your chances of reuniting with your lover with more flowers. A combination of lavender and marigold is said to be effective when casting your love spell. With your intention, mix these flowers in the right proportions to create a powder and use it for your lover's spell rituals.

- **Powder of sympathy** is a common ingredient used to speed up the love magic spell. It aligns the energies within the caster and the target to make the process faster.

- **Photos**: the spell caster will need your lover's photo or the two of you together.

- **Lovers' return oil**: Love oil can also be used to bring back your lost lover. Pick the flowers when the moon is waxing to make your spell more powerful.

- **Hair strands**: Get a strand of your lover's hair since this is an essential ingredient for casting a spell to bring your lover back. You can look for your lover's hair on a comb or follow them to hair salons.

- **Ex-lover's clothes**: a piece of your lover's clothing is another essential ingredient you should get for a love spell to be successful.

- **Nail clippings** can produce a powerful spell and play a pivotal role in bringing back your lover. However, it might be difficult for you to get these components, so see how best you can get them.

- **Jewelry** is another magical ingredient for your love spell to return an ex-lover. It should not be a very expensive piece, so an old ring or bracelet will suffice.

However, there are certain things you should never do even if you manage to get all the ingredients. For instance, you should never cast a spell to make your ex-lover stay with you against their will. Your spells should brick someone to the place where they want to be and not be forced. The other person should be ready for the love that comes with the spell.

If possible, you need to consult your ex-lover and let them know your intentions, so you don't take them by surprise. When it comes to love matters, never force things as it may produce undesired results. You need to set your differences aside with your lover if you want to enjoy your relationship once you reconcile.

Magic

Irish pagans also practice magic like other religions. Witchcraft was prohibited in Ireland and Scotland, but this later changed around the 18th Century. When honoring their deities, witches believe humans have the power to cause a change in different forms that cannot be proved by science. Witches also perform rituals and spells to heal people and help them with general life issues. Magic should never be performed to harm someone, and the following are positive examples.

Candle Magic

This is a good general-purpose spell anyone can do as long as they believe in it. You need to pick a candle with the right color for the job you want to undertake. For example, yellow represents wealth, pink or green for love, blue for good fortune, red for strength, brown for stability, and mauve for wisdom. If you wish to attract something, write its name from the candle's top to the bottom. Conversely, you can also write what you want to dispel from the bottom to the top of the candle.

Like other types of magic, it is best to do your candle magic after dark. It is a good idea to begin your magic on a new moon if you want to draw something to yourself. On the other hand, begin the spell on a waning moon if you want to dispel something. Light the candle and visualize what you want to achieve, and maintain your concentration. Blow out the candle when you finish and repeat the procedure the following night until the moon passes the waning or waxing stage. When you are done, bury the candle somewhere and don't throw it away. Forget about the spell, and don't talk about it.

Witches' Poppets

Poppets are wax, clay, or plasticine figures resembling the person you want the magic to focus on. When consecrated on the witch's altar, the poppet can be attached by a cord to a man and woman. A combination of female and male energy is believed to be most effective and provides symbolic treatment. The poppet's leg can be bandaged as part of the healing spell. The mouth can also be sewn closed to prevent the living person represented by the poppet from spreading gossip.

When the ritual has worked or achieved its goals, the poppet is buried or burned to release the spell. Essentially, when you undertake a particular spell, you'll be communicating with invisible spirits, and they will hear you as long as you do the right thing. If you think you want to heal someone, get the appropriate tools for the spell or ritual. It is crucial to visualize your intention and what you want to achieve when performing the spell to make it effective.

Spells for Protection

You must learn about your environment wherever you live and understand the folklore of the area. Honor the spirits of the land and seek energy from sacred sites honored by the people who lived before you. Weave your energy and relationship with the spirits of the earth for protection against evil spells. For example, Rowan trees are used for protection. There are also other trees with equivalent properties in other parts of the world. You must know how they can protect you against evil spells.

Look for a rowan tree and honor it as an ally by asking for a gift of the tree's wood or berries. Thread the berries into a bracelet to wear when you feel you need protection. You can also put rowan twig crosses tied with a red cord at your windows and doors to protect you. Make sure you thank the tree for the charms. Create a landscape where you can plant a single tree and treat it as a sacred space to perform your rituals. The spirits will recognize all the efforts you make to connect with nature. You must perform your rituals regularly to enjoy unlimited protection.

Healing Rites

You should understand and honor the water sources around you if you want to perform healing rites. The traditional folk healing method requires you to visit a holy well or sacred body of water and dip a cloth in the water. Wash the sick person while at the same time asking the spirits of the water to cure and bless them. Leave the cloth on a hawthorn tree and leave it to biodegrade. As the cloth rots, the illness is taken away from the sick patient. The process should happen naturally for the best results.

This practice is known as hanging clooties, and some people often misunderstand it. You should use biodegradable cloth, so the tree's growth is not affected. When something is bad for the land or nature, it is not good for folk magic. Therefore, using plastic or other non-biodegradable material may not give you positive results from your spell. Plastic impacts the environment in many ways since it does not rot like other compostable matter, so you should not include it in your spells if you want to achieve your goals.

Irish Paganism emphasizes the significance of developing close links with nature and achieved through different rites. This chapter discussed different pagan spells and rituals to help people resolve different aspects of their lives. Before undertaking these spells, it is essential to know the ingredients required and how to use them. Make sure you follow the instructions or enlist the services of an experienced practitioner.

Conclusion

After an overview of the Pagan history in Ireland, it becomes clear that Irish Paganism represents the perfect blend of ancient traditions, modern adaptations, and beliefs adopted from other religions. Due to the endless devotions of the Druids, many traditional practices remained, even in modern Irish Paganism. Followers are still free to choose their spiritual guides – whether a deity or any other creature inhabiting the natural realms. In many religions, only loyalty and honesty are emphasized as character traits to aim for. On the other hand, Pagans also believe in personal responsibility. Pagans honor their deities and spiritual guides with festivals and rituals and highlight the importance of respecting nature and its energy. Each solstice on the Witches Wheel of the Year holds a unique significance to the Celts' life. They are all related to events at specific times of the year.

Learning about Celtic spirituality will allow you to unlock the secrets of Druidry in Ireland along with the Welsh witchcraft practices. Many overlaps between Irish and Welsh witchcraft occur, but the latter is known for its unique characteristic, such as the four branches of belief. Due to being nature-based, Celtic witchcraft was more popular and widespread in Ireland than in any other country, allowing the Welsh branches to differentiate from it. In times of need, the spirits and the deities that followers turn to are also different for

Irish and Welsh Pagans. While Paganism wasn't always associated with witchcraft, the local folk beliefs and healing practices in Ireland made it much easier for the connection to form between these two customs.

Nowadays, many ancient Paganism practices are long gone, and those that survived were only able to with the help of Druidry. Despite the Celts' oppression following the spread of Christianity in Ireland and the subsequent loss of influence they endured, the Druids managed to pass parts of the Celtic tradition to the next generations. Due to their efforts, even in modern times, the ancient legacy of Paganism is still alive - albeit mostly in neopaganism, and other similar contemporary Pagan beliefs, such as Wicca.

Lastly, this book empowered you with knowledge about magickal tools and their uses in Irish Paganism. Whether you are just learning the way of the witch or are well versed in spiritual practices, using the proper tools will make you better in your craft. Setting up an altar isn't always required for becoming an active practitioner, but having a sacred space will enhance your ability to cast an intention and make your wishes become a reality. An altar can be dedicated to the preferred deity and serve as a surface to prepare everything you need to perform a spell or a ritual. With so many candles, crystals, wands, and incantations to choose from, your sacred space will inspire you to find the perfect combination leading you down the right path whenever you need an answer or guidance in your practice.

Here's another book by Mari Silva that you might like

Your Free Gift (only available for a limited time)

Thanks for getting this book! If you want to learn more about various spirituality topics, then join Mari Silva's community and get a free guided meditation MP3 for awakening your third eye. This guided meditation mp3 is designed to open and strengthen ones third eye so you can experience a higher state of consciousness. Simply visit the link below the image to get started.

https://spiritualityspot.com/meditation

References

O'Reilly, L. J. (2020, May 7). Paganism: Ireland's contemporary shining light. Trinity News.

http://trinitynews.ie/2020/05/paganism-irelands-contemporary-shining-light

Irish Pagan beliefs. (2018, September 25). Lora O'Brien - Irish Author & Guide.

https://loraobrien.ie/irish-pagan-belief

Celtic religion - Beliefs, practices, and institutions. (n.d.). In Encyclopedia Britannica.

Culture Northern Ireland. (n.d.). Irish pagan gods. Culture Northern Ireland.

https://www.culturenorthernireland.org/features/heritage/irish-pagan-gods

Daimler, M. (2015). Irish Paganism: Reconstructing Irish polytheism. Moon Books.

Irish Pagan beliefs. (2018, September 25). Lora O'Brien - Irish Author & Guide.

https://loraobrien.ie/irish-pagan-beliefs

Joyce, P. W. (2018). The story of ancient Irish civilization. Outlook Verlag.

O'Reilly, L. J. (2020, May 7). Paganism: Ireland's contemporary shining light. Trinity News. http://trinitynews.ie/2020/05/paganism-irelands-contemporary-shining-light

Pizza, M., & Lewis, J. (Eds.). (2008). Handbook of contemporary Paganism. Brill Academic. https://doi.org/10.1163/ej.9789004163737.i-650

The snakes are still in Ireland: Pagans, shamans, and modern Druids in a catholic world. (2013, May 10). The On Being Project. https://onbeing.org/blog/the-snakes-are-still-in-ireland-pagans-shamans-and-modern-Druids-in-a-catholic-world

Top gods and goddesses from Celtic mythology. (2021, December 30). IrishCentral.Com. https://www.irishcentral.com/roots/history/celtic-mythology-gods-goddesses

Cartwright, M. (2021). Druid. World History Encyclopedia. https://www.worldhistory.org/Druid

Who were the Druids? (2017, March 21). Historic UK.

https://www.historic-uk.com/HistoryUK/HistoryofWales/Druids

A day in the life of a Celtic Druid - Philip Freeman. (2019, September 17). TED-Ed.

Crawford, C. (2020, July 14). A beginners guide to the Wheel of the Year – . The Self-Care Emporium. https://theselfcareemporium.com/blog/beginners-guide-wheel-of-the-year

The Pagan Grimoire. (2020, April 18). Wheel of the Year: The 8 Wiccan sabbats (2021 + 2022 dates). The Pagan Grimoire. https://www.pagangrimoire.com/wheel-of-the-year

Barry, B. (2017, October 12). What sparked our fear of witches – and what kept it burning so long? Washington Post (Washington, D.C.:

1974). https://www.washingtonpost.com/entertainment/books/what-sparked-our-fear-of-witches--and-what-kept-it-burning-so-long

Bradley, C. (2020, December 23). "pagan" vs. "Wicca": What is the difference? Dictionary.com website: https://www.dictionary.com/e/pagan-vs-wicca-pagan-vs-heathen

Lewis, I. M., & Russell, J. B. (2021). witchcraft. In Encyclopedia Britannica.

SelFelin, Fields, K., John, Ben, Medieval Magic: Alchemy, Witchery, and Magic from the Middle Ages, Jennifer, ... Morganwg, R. (2019, June 17). Welsh goddesses and gods: List and descriptions + how to honor them. Otherworldly Oracle website:

https://otherworldlyoracle.com/welsh-goddesses-gods

witchcraft - The witch hunts. (n.d.). In Encyclopedia Britannica.

Little, B. (2018, January 10). How medieval churches used witch hunts to gain more followers. HISTORY website: https://www.history.com/news/how-medieval-churches-used-witch-hunts-to-gain-more-followers

Celtic god of blacksmithing and hospitality goibniu. (n.d.). Worldanvil.Com.

https://www.worldanvil.com/w/tyran-jackswiftshot/a/celtic-god-of-blacksmithing-and-hospitality-goibniu-article

Gill, N. S. (n.d.). A list of Celtic gods and goddesses. ThoughtCo.

https://www.thoughtco.com/celtic-gods-and-goddesses-117625

Heritage, E. (2017, October 31). Legendary Irish Gods and Goddesses. Emerald Heritage. https://emerald-heritage.com/blog/2017/legendary-irish-gods-and-goddesses

Klimczak, N. (2021, June 4). Aine: Radiant Celtic goddess of love, summer, and sovereignty. Ancient-Origins.Net; Ancient Origins. https://www.ancient-origins.net/myths-legends/aine-radiant-celtic-goddess-007097

Mandal, D. (2018, July 2). 15 ancient Celtic gods and goddesses you should know about. Realm of History. https://www.realmofhistory.com/2018/07/02/ancient-celtic-gods-goddesses-facts

Perkins, M. (n.d.). Irish mythology: History and legacy. ThoughtCo. http://thoughtco.com/irish-mythology-4768762

The call of Danu. (n.d.). The Call of Danu. https://thecallofdanu.wordpress.com

The Celtic god Nuada. (n.d.). Thecottagemystic.Com. https://www.thecottagemystic.com/nuada.html

Whitecatgrove, V. A. P. (2010, July 27). Invocations to Goibhniu and Manannan. White Cat Grove. https://whitecatgrove.wordpress.com/2010/07/27/invocations-to-goibhniu-and-manannan

Williams, A. (2020, August 16). Cu Chulainn. Mythopedia. https://mythopedia.com/topics/cu-chulainn

Dewey, P. (2020, April 10). The story of The Mabinogion and its impact on Welsh literature and beyond. WalesOnline website: https://www.walesonline.co.uk/whats-on/arts-culture-news/story-mabinogion-impact-welsh-literature-18040842

SelFelin, Fields, K., John, Ben, Medieval Magic: Alchemy, Witchery, and Magic from the Middle Ages, Jennifer, ... Morganwg, R. (2019, June 17). Welsh goddesses and gods: List and descriptions + how to honor them. Otherworldly Oracle website:

https://otherworldlyoracle.com/welsh-goddesses-gods

Why mythology is still important today. (n.d.). Parmaobserver.com website:

http://www.parmaobserver.com/read/2013/02/01/why-mythology-is-still-important-today

20 modern traditions with pagan origins. (2019, September 5). TheEssentialBS.Com. https://theessentialbs.com/2019/09/05/20-modern-traditions-with-pagan-origins

John Halstead, C. (2015, October 2). We're not all Witches: An introduction to Neopaganism. HuffPost. https://www.huffpost.com/entry/were-not-all-witches-an-i_b_8228434

Wigington, P. (n.d.). The magic & symbolism of animals. Learn Religions.

https://www.learnreligions.com/the-magic-of-animals-2562522

An Irish Pagan Altar - Lora O'Brien - Irish author & guide. (2018, October 22). Retrieved, from Lora O'Brien - Irish Author & Guide website: https://loraobrien.ie/irish-pagan-altar

Celtic Wicca altar setup. (n.d.). Deviantart.com website:

https://www.deviantart.com/morsoth/art/Celtic-Wicca-Altar-Setup-539056829?comment=1%3A539056829%3A3879380538

The Goddess movement. (n.d.).

https://www.bbc.co.uk/religion/religions/paganism/subdivisions/goddess.shtml

The Irish Times. (2000, January 22). Something Wiccan this way comes. Irish Times. https://www.irishtimes.com/news/something-wiccan-this-way-comes-1.236955

McGarry, M. (2020, April 30). Fire, water, light, and luck: Bealtaine traditions in Ireland. RTÉ website: https://www.rte.ie/brainstorm/2019/0429/1046282-fire-water-light-and-luck-bealtaine-traditions-in-ireland

Gardner, P. (2016). Wicca: The pan Gardner book of shadows - A spiritual guide to spells, rituals, and Wiccan traditions. North Charleston, SC: CreateSpace Independent Publishing Platform.

Key ingredients to use for spells to bring someone back. (n.d.). Org. UK website:

https://rfs.org.uk/articles/key_ingredients_to_use_for_spells_to_bring_someone_back.html

Claddagh Design. (2022, January 19). Celtic festivals: What is Bealtaine? Claddaghdesign.com website: https://www.claddaghdesign.com/history/all-about-bealtaine

Guardian staff reporter. (2000, October 28). The witching hour. The Guardian. https://www.theguardian.com/theguardian/2000/oct/28/weekend7.weekend3

Irish Pagan beliefs. (2018, September 25). Lora O'Brien - Irish Author & Guide. https://loraobrien.ie/irish-pagan-beliefs

O'Reilly, L. J. (2020, May 7). Paganism: Ireland's contemporary shining light. Trinity News. http://trinitynews.ie/2020/05/paganism-irelands-contemporary-shining-light

Morissette, A. (2015, October 11). Top 10 tools of divination. Alanis Morissette website: https://alanis.com/news/top-10-tools-of-divination

Wigington, P. (n.d.). 14 magical tools for pagan practice. Learn Religions website: https://www.learnreligions.com/magical-tools-for-pagan-practice-4064607